Nationalist Responses to the Crises in Europe

The last few years have witnessed a remarkable resurgence of populist nationalism as indicated by Brexit, the Trump presidency and the rise of radical parties of the far right. *Nationalist Responses to the Crises in Europe* examines the drivers, methods and local appeal of populist nationalism. Based on multi-sited fieldwork in England, Hungary and Norway, Cathrine Thorleifsson explores the various material conditions, historical events and social contexts that shape distinct forms of xenophobia and intolerance toward migrants and minorities. Combining analysis of the discourses propagated by populist radical right parties like the UK Independence Party, Fidesz, Jobbik and the Norwegian Progress Party with an analysis of the fears and concerns of supporters, Thorleifsson develops wider conclusions about the drivers and character of populist nationalism and the way in which these differ across national contexts. An empirically grounded study of how the demand and supply sides of populist nationalism are reconfigured in response to the globalized crises of economy, culture and displacement, this book will appeal to scholars of anthropology, sociology and politics with interests in nationalism, populism, the radical right and contemporary xenophobia.

Cathrine Thorleifsson is a researcher at the Centre for Research on Extremism at the University of Oslo, Norway. She earned a PhD in Anthropology from the London School of Economics and Political Science in 2012, and from 2014–2017 she was a postdoctoral fellow at the ERC-funded project 'Overheating: The Three Crises of Globalization'. She is the author of *Nationalism and the Politics of Fear in Israel: Race and Identity on the Border with Lebanon* (2015).

Research in Migration and Ethnic Relations Series
Series Editor: Maykel Verkuyten, ERCOMER Utrecht University

The Research in Migration and Ethnic Relations series has been at the forefront of research in the field for ten years. The series has built an international reputation for cutting edge theoretical work, for comparative research especially on Europe and for nationally-based studies with broader relevance to international issues. Published in association with the European Research Centre on Migration and Ethnic Relations (ERCOMER), Utrecht University, it draws contributions from the best international scholars in the field, offering an interdisciplinary perspective on some of the key issues of the contemporary world.

Diasporas and Homeland Conflicts
A Comparative Perspective Challenges
Bahar Baser

Intercultural Education in the European Context
Theories, Experiences, Challenges
Marco Catarci, Massimiliano Fiorucci

The Migration of Highly Educated Turkish Citizens to Europe
From Guestworkers to Global Talent
Zeynep Yanasmayan

Nationalist Responses to the Crisis in Europe
Old and New Hatreds
Cathrine Thorleifsson

For more information about this series, please visit: https://www.routledge.com/sociology/series/ASHSER1136

Nationalist Responses to the Crises in Europe
Old and New Hatreds

Cathrine Thorleifsson

LONDON AND NEW YORK

First published 2019
by Routledge
2 Park Square, Milton Park, Abingdon, Oxon OX14 4RN

52 Vanderbilt Avenue, New York, NY 10017

First issued in paperback 2020

Routledge is an imprint of the Taylor & Francis Group, an informa business

© 2019 Cathrine Thorleifsson

The right of Cathrine Thorleifsson to be identified as author of this work has been asserted by her in accordance with sections 77 and 78 of the Copyright, Designs and Patents Act 1988.

All rights reserved. No part of this book may be reprinted or reproduced or utilised in any form or by any electronic, mechanical, or other means, now known or hereafter invented, including photocopying and recording, or in any information storage or retrieval system, without permission in writing from the publishers.

Trademark notice: Product or corporate names may be trademarks or registered trademarks, and are used only for identification and explanation without intent to infringe.

British Library Cataloguing in Publication Data
A catalogue record for this book is available from the British Library

Library of Congress Cataloging-in-Publication Data
Names: Thorleifsson, Cathrine, author.
Title: Nationalist responses to the crises in Europe : old and new hatreds / Cathrine Thorleifsson.Description: Abingdon, Oxon ; New York, NY : Routledge, 2019. |
Series: Research in migration and ethnic relations series | Includes bibliographical references and index.
Identifiers: LCCN 2018025201| ISBN 9781472466471 (hbk) | ISBN 9781315597478 (ebk)
Subjects: LCSH: Nationalism--Europe. | Populism--Europe. | Right-wing extremists--Europe. | Xenophobia--Europe. | Europe--Ethnic relations.
Classification: LCC JC311 .T64 2019 | DDC 320.54094--dc23
LC record available at https://lccn.loc.gov/2018025201

ISBN 13: 978-0-36-758506-8 (pbk)
ISBN 13: 978-1-4724-6647-1 (hbk)

Typeset in Times New Roman
by Taylor & Francis Books

To Ragna, Rikke and Tobias, for your enduring love and support.

Contents

List of figures	viii
Preface	ix
Abbreviations	xii

Introduction: Rupture and resentment in twenty-first-century Europe		1
1	From coal to Ukip: The struggle over identity in post-industrial Doncaster	11
2	In pursuit of purity: Populism and the politics of whiteness	34
3	Disposable strangers: Far-right securitization of migration in Hungary	47
4	The Swedish dystopia: Violent imaginaries of the radical right	75
5	Human waste in the land of abundance: Prejudice and ambivalence towards itinerant Roma	89
Conclusion		101

References	105
Index	113

Figures

1.1	A Polish shop in Doncaster	16
1.2	A pound shop in Doncaster	17
2.1	'Out of the EU and into the world'	39
2.2	'Pan-European Migrant Rape Story'	43
3.1	An old steel factory in Ózd	55
3.2	Jobbik rally in Budapest	67
3.3	The alternative Holocaust memorial at Szabadság Square consisting of personal items, family photos, books and documents, built by children and grandchildren of Holocaust survivors	71
4.1	Neo-Nazis at a Jobbik rally	85

Preface

Writing this book has been the result of four years' research. When I began the project on the rise of populist nationalism, the background was the economic crisis in Europe. I wanted to explore and compare the material and socio-cultural contexts in places where populist radical right (PRR) parties had obtained their electoral breakthrough. How did the global crisis affect local life worlds and what were the concerns and aspirations of supporters of populist nationalism? While I was conducting fieldwork in England and Hungary in the late summer of 2015, another 'crisis' affected Europe, the so-called refugee 'crisis'. The influx of asylum seekers to Europe reached an unprecedented level with some 885,000 migrants arriving. That year alone an estimated 3,800 refugees and migrants lost their lives in the attempt to cross the Mediterranean to reach the shores of Europe. What was a humanitarian crisis and crisis of cooperation in the European Union, was framed in radical right discourse as a crisis of security and national identity for Europe.

Because social reality is never static, researching the way humans make sense out of their lives in response to contemporary forces and events is like researching a constantly moving target. Acknowledging the uneven speed and scale of accelerated change, this book thus attempts to analyse the rise and appeal of populist nationalism in response to the interrelated crises of economy and displacement. It uses social science perspectives on nationalism, globalization and identity, with original empirical material to examine how the boundaries of the nation are reconfigured by radical right parties, politicians and their supporters.

While an analysis of economic contexts and PRR discourses online has been key from a methodological perpective, this book could not have materialized without the generous time of all the people I have met in the course of my research for it. First, I extend my gratitude to the people I met in England, Hungary and Norway, for sharing their stories, experiences and for allowing me into their professional and private lives. In total I spent six months in the field, spending considerable time with ordinary supporters of anti-immigration PRR parties. While I have had previous experience living with people whose political convictions I do not necessarily share (my previous book was on nationalism in Israel and entailed fieldwork amongst supporters of the radical right parties Likud and Shas), I was still anxious about access and how I would be received. I acknowledge that my own biography, as a 32-year-old white, female postdoctoral researcher from Norway, and middle class, affected my informants' pronouncement. However, my outsider status might have gained me an enhanced level of trust and possibly the people I met felt less restrained in their discussions. Access was much less of a challenge than I initially had envisioned. People were largely not suspicious, and were open and eager to share their hopes, fears and concerns with someone who was interested in their lives and had the time to listen.

The role of being an emphatic listener – yet critical researcher – can be a difficult balancing act. While they might not agree with my analysis of the information they shared, I thank the leadership of the UK Independence Party (Ukip) and Jobbik – Movement for a better Hungary – for providing me with generous access to their conferences, meetings and campaigns. In England, I thank in particular Gawain Towler, Ukip's former press officer, for giving me access to the Ukip conference, which gave valuable insights into the party culture and themes mobilized by political elites. In Hungary, I thank Jobbik Vice President Daniel Kárpát for allowing me access to the party's campaign against migration. I informed him about the purpose of the study and obtained verbal consent to use his full name. I respected all key elite informants' wishes to have their identity acknowledged or kept confidential, where the majority chose the former. I might have gained access to the parties owing to their belief that I would produce flattering party portraits. However, combining close interpretations of my interlocutors' narratives and practices with a critical approach has been important from a methodological point of view. I have strived to let the people I met remain in focus without reproducing their nationalist discourses.

I express my sincere gratitude to Thomas Hylland Eriksen at the Department of Anthropology at the University of Oslo, for mentorship and support. In 2014, I became a member of his ERC Advanced Grant project 'Overheating: The Three Crises of Globalization, or an anthropological history of the early 21st century', together with colleagues Elisabeth Schober, Robert Pijpers, Lena Gross, Henrik Sindig-Larsen, Wim Van Daele, Astrid Stensrud and Chris Hann. Eriksen's theoretical visions combined with generous intellectual exchange with the research group has been a constant source of inspiration. The fifth chapter developed from a joint essay written together with Eriksen in 2017 and I thank him for his valuable contribution in thinking through key concepts.

I am grateful for the many comments and criticisms I have received presenting chapters at conferences such as the European Association for Social Anthropology (EASA) and the American Anthropological Association (AAA). Throughout the project, I have also benefited from ongoing conversations and fellowship with researchers at the newly established Centre for Research on Extremism (C-REX). In particular, conversations with Anders Ravik Jupskås and Cas Mudde have influenced my thinking. I would like to thank the following for having provided me with advice and direction at critical stages during fieldwork: Mária M. Kovács Margit Feischmidt, Kristóf Szombati, Peter Krekó, Adam Bihari and Matthew Goodwin.

I gratefully acknowledge the institutions that funded this project. The Norwegian Research Council (NFR) provided two years' funding for 2014–2016. C-REX with funds from NFR provided funding for a subsequent year, ensuring the material security and institutional support needed to complete the manuscript. I thank assistant editor Alice Salt at Routledge who was attendant to all details as she skilfully and efficiently guided the book through production. Finally, I owe a debt of gratitude to my husband Tobias Thorleifsson for pushing and sustaining me as well as being a constant for our daughters Ragna and Rikke. You all bore the brunt of my determination to complete this book, and I am wholeheartedly grateful for your sacrifice, support and patience. All my love goes out to you.

Abbreviations

AFD	Alternative for Germany Party
EU	European Union
FPÖ	Austrian Freedom Party
ISIS	Islamic State in Iraq and Syria
LSE	London School of Economics and Political Science
MEP	member of the European Parliament
MP	member of Parliament
NGO	non-governmental organization
PiS	Law and Justice Party
PRR	populist radical right
PVV	Dutch Freedom Party
Q&A	questions and answers
SD	Sweden Democrats
Ukip	UK Independence Party

Introduction
Rupture and resentment in twenty-first-century Europe

The last few years have witnessed a remarkable pan-European and transatlantic resurgence of nationalism as indicated by the UK's decision to leave the European Union (EU), known as 'Brexit', and the Trump presidency. Populist radical right (PRR) parties have received unprecedented double-digit support on a Eurosceptic and anti-immigration platform. In 2017, Marine Le Pen made it to the second round of the French presidential elections. The Alternative for Germany party (AFD) won 13 per cent of the vote in the 2017 federal elections and in 2018 it was polling above the Social Democrats. In Austria, the Austrian Freedom Party (FPÖ), a party with roots in fascism, has entered the governing coalition. In Hungary, the authoritarian Prime Minister Viktor Orbán has embraced ethnic nationalism, challenging the basic values and principles underlying both liberal democracy and the EU.

Adopting a critical ethnographic approach, this book examines the causes, dynamics and appeal of populist nationalisms in contemporary Europe. Addressing gaps in state of the art, the book offers fresh empirical data and much-needed insight into the motivations and concerns of supporters of the populist radical right. Drawing on multi-sited fieldwork carried out in England, Hungary and Norway amongst the voters and supporters of the UK Independence Party, Fidesz and Jobbik, and the Progress Party, it explores the various historical events, material conditions and socio-cultural contexts that shape resistance towards migrants and diversity. Examining multiple sites across countries, I argue that the rise and appeal of populist nationalism must be analysed in relation to increasing economic and cultural insecurities linked to globalization. Processes of economic and state transition, diversification and migration have affected states and regions unevenly. The uncertainties and societal ruptures associated with globalization have enabled the heating of populist nationalisms in local struggles over resources and recognition.

Analysing the practices and discourses of PRR parties and politicians, I demonstrate what tropes and themes the elite nationalists mobilize across national contexts. I find that although the PRR parties vary in history, ideology and orientation, they all frame migrants and minorities, particularly Muslims, as fundamentally threatening to national identity, culture and security. In particular, the current radical right externalization of migrants from Muslim-majority lands as human waste or 'exception populations' (Agamben 2005) is strikingly similar across national contexts. The so-called refugee crisis has been exploited by radical right parties to fuel anti-immigration and anti-Islam sentiments. Le Pen, Orbán and Trump have all, through xenophobic electoral campaigns, marked Muslim migrants as the defining Other. Using nationalist rhetoric and imaginaries that reinforce a sense of threat, they warn against 'illegal' strangers who are invading the nation while presenting themselves as protectors of a nation and Christian civilization in danger.

While considering the part that political leaders play in shaping populist nationalism, I pay special attention to how these discourses and imaginaries are consumed or contested by ordinary supporters as they reproduce ethnic, national and racialized forms of collective belonging in their everyday life. This introductory chapter will present the main concepts, theoretical and methodological approaches to be used throughout the book. It also explores theoretical shortcomings in the state of the art and shows how a multi-sited ethno-methodological approach can reveal new insights into the appeal, dynamics and character of populist nationalism.

Culture, economy or both?

The chief focus of the book is on exclusionary nationalism that together with authoritarianism and populism are core features of populist radical right parties. Exclusionary nationalism, also referred to in the literature as nativism, is an ideology that holds that states should be inhabited by members of the native group ('the nation'), and that non-native people and ideas are fundamentally threatening to the homogenous nation-state (Mudde and Kaltwasser 2017). Nationalism is the project to make the political unit, the state (or polity) congruent with the cultural unit, the nation (Fox and Miller-Indriss 2008). Nationalism operates through notions of an 'authentic' and pure nation that is continuously re-narrated (Bhabha 1990), re-imagined (Anderson 1991) and re-invented (Hobsbawm 1991) in relation to differentiated others.

While populism is a secondary concern of my analysis, as I use it intermittently the contested and slippery concept still requires clear defining. Following Mudde and Kaltwasser (2017), I approach populism as an ideology or political discourse which 'considers society to be ultimately separated into two homogenous and antagonistic groups – "the pure people" versus the "corrupt elite", and which argues that politics should be an expression of the "volonté générale" (general will) of the people'. Populism's 'thinness' is a product of the vagueness of its core concepts which allows it to be combined with 'thick' ideologies such as socialism and nationalism (Mudde 2004:543, Urbinati 2014:131). For the sake of conceptual clarity, I will in the book define populist nationalism as the exclusionary and polarizing nationalism that pits morally 'pure' and virtuous insiders against a set of internal and external others who are depicted as threatening to the nation-state.

PRR parties' gain of power calls for a thorough examination of the conditions that have led to their rise. Based on a review of the multi-disciplinary literature across political science, sociology, history, cultural and media studies, and anthropology, one can define multiple general approaches related to the rise and character of nationalism in Europe and beyond. Scholars have shown how nationalism can emerge in response to the outcomes of globalization such as migration and diversification processes (Ivarsflaten and Gudrandsen 2014), global capitalism (Holmes 2000), the threat and actuality of terrorism (Jurgensmeyer 2003), and the spread of new information technology (Eriksen 2016, Wodak 2015). A major focus in the literature has been on the effects of neoliberal restructuring of capital accumulation and state transformation on the rise of nationalism linking the rise of anti-immigration PRR parties to working-class and gendered resentment of economic insecurity (Kalb and Halmani 2011, Pirro 2014, Rudgren and Ruth 2013, Hann 2015). Other scholars have critiqued the 'losers of globalization' thesis showing how supporters from a range of class backgrounds can be drawn to parties and movements propagating protectionist nationalism for a variety of reasons, including political discontent (Van Kessel 2011), resistance to immigration and diversification (Ivarsflaten 2008), the affirmation of identity, masculinity, personal loyalties and nostalgia for a past lost (Fangen 1999, Blee 2002, Kimmel 2003, Mudde 2007, Müller 2016, Hochschild 2018).

A growing body of research contests the weight put on material conditions. Indeed, it was primarily the left-wing anti-austerity populist parties (Syriza in Greece and Podemos in Spain) that used the sovereign debt crisis as an opportunity to reframe economic conflict in nationalist terms. The rise of the Swedish Democrats (2014) and Progress Party in Norway is not a direct result of the economic crisis, but can be interpreted in terms of the long-term tendencies undermining conventional parties in general and social-democratic parties in particular, the latter of which have plummeted across European contexts. Several scholars argue that cultural, and not economic, insecurity is the driving force of populist nationalism (Norris and Inglehart 2016, Kaufman 2018). Fukuyama, who predicted that liberal democracy represented 'the end of history', notes in the description of his forthcoming book (2018) that populist nationalism, said to be rooted in economic motivation, actually springs from the demand for recognition and therefore cannot simply be satisfied by economic means.

Despite the scholarly disagreement over what the main driving forces of populist nationalism are, what appears evident is that PRR parties have captured a segment of the population's fears and insecurities about the impact of immigration and increasingly ethno-cultural and religious diversity on identity (Wodak 2015), promising firm boundaries in the face of transnational flows of people and ideas (Gullestad, in Gingrich and Banks 2006:83). This aligns with the findings from several studies that suggest that citizens feel threatened by migration, and are suspicious of or hostile towards ethnic 'out groups' (Goodwin and Ford 2014, Berezin 2009, Mudde 2007), perceived as posing a threat to the nation imagined as homogenous (Barker 1981, Gilroy 1987, 2000). The label of the 'radical' thus refers to the resistance towards immigration and the nativist rejection of diversity expressed at the (far) right end of the political spectrum (Akkerman et al. 2016).

A multi-sited study of populist nationalism

In the book, I argue that the resurgence and appeal of populist nationalism cannot be reduced to one single crisis and driving factor (culture or economy), but must be analysed in relation to the combined effects of the converging crisis of twenty-first-century Europe – economy, displacement, culture and identity (Eriksen 2016b). The outcomes of globalization such as the rise of global capitalism and growing inequality (Pikkety 2014), mass immigration and demographic change, can be seen as constituting what Eriksen refers to as an overheating effect (Eriksen 2016). As a metaphor, overheating refers to the acceleration and intensification of global processes since the early 1990s. While change, development and progress have been hailed as positive ideals, Eriksen notes that there is 'something new and sinister about the contemporary, speed, scope and scale of change today. The change is out of control and the (un)-intended consequences can be devastating' (Eriksen 2016, 2016b). The rise of PRR parties can thus be analysed as political attempts to scale down processes of globalization, and seek cultural and economic protectionism against contemporary forces perceived as threatening.

The aims of this book are to provide theoretical insights and empirical knowledge on the thoughts, appeal, methods and goals of nationalists and how these are reconfigured in relation to the interrelated crisis of globalization: the crisis of economy and displacement. While these crises are global in character, they entail local effects and responses. The analytical focus is accordingly located to the space between discursive socio-cultural constructions and the actual material conditions on the basis of which they are constructed (Eriksen 2016).

In order to get detailed insights into the wide varieties of local responses to the interrelated crises of economy, culture and migration, I conducted ethnographic research in England, Hungary and Norway in 2015, in countries with differences in history, experiences with immigration and level of impact by the recession. I designed the research agenda to examine the dynamics of populist nationalism across multiple sites and societal scales, connecting individual experiences with the broader historical, political, socio-economic and cultural environment in which they are embedded. I identified the local set of conditions and circumstances conducive to the rise and appeal of populist nationalist discourses, and exclusionary myths and practices about minorities and migrants.

A central dimension of populist nationalism examined in the book is the so-called supply side – and what narrative strategies, imaginaries and discourses are propagated by PRR parties and politicians. Several scholars have demonstrated ways to study populist nationalist ideology based on an analysis of the discursive pattern of political texts (see Rooduijn 2014, Rooduijn and Pauwels 2011). PRR parties are eclectically synthesizing elements from different ideologies and traditions in local, regional and national resistance to diversity and migration, whether expressed in religious or secular, ethnic, national or gendered terms (Kimmel 2003, Yuval-Davis 1997). Feminist scholars have noted how discourses and practices pertaining to gender are integral to neo-nationalist ideology (Moghadam 1994, Yuval-Davis 1997, Kimmel 2003, Nagel 2010), and media scholars have showed how meaning from other transnational contexts reconfigure grammars of exclusion online (Fairclough 2003, Wodak 2015).

The examination of the discourses propagated by PRR parties and their supporters is relevant for understanding the appeal of their supply side. Moreover, examining practices and discourses can reveal some of the ways in which the populist radical right re-narrate (Bhabha 1990), re-imagine (Anderson 1991) and re-invent the boundaries of the nation. Through qualitative content analysis of data from discourses (Wodak 1999), I present evidence of what gendered, religious or nationalist tropes are mobilized by PRR parties. The parties I have researched are the UK Independence Party (Ukip), Fidesz and Jobbik, and the Progress Party. In addition I have analysed some of the discourse and practices propagated by the Sweden Democrats and the Trump presidential campaign as these parties literally entered my field site as collaborators of Ukip. I acknowledge that these parties and actors differ significantly in their origins and ideological orientation. The Norwegian Progress Party and Ukip are not nearly as radical as Fidesz or the ultra-nationalist Jobbik, shorthand for Jobbik Magyarországért Mozgalom—Movement for a Better Hungary, in Hungary, which both embrace ethnic nationalism. While the parties and political campaigns I analyse represent different ideological types and 'degrees' (Pauwels 2011) of the radical right, I suggest that they converge in their methods and concerns, in particular when it comes to how they frame migrants or minorities as threatening others to the nation. Materials for this research included myriad platforms such as party events, campaigns, manifestos, speeches and websites. In addition I have examined online materials and news articles that promote the causes of PRR actors.

Populist nationalist thought and practice are never static, but constantly adjusting to new transnational and global conditions (Gingrich and Banks 2006, Eriksen 2016), societal developments and critical events. Against the general background of globalized crises, new communication channels and technologies are used by PRR actors that contribute to the opportunity for nationalist mobilization. PRR politicians routinely make use of social media to promote their image and disseminate ideas or the 'truths' that they accuse mainstream media of hiding from 'the people'. In the UK and Norway, I have analysed content in open-access social media platforms such as Facebook and

6   *Introduction*

Twitter. Based on online fieldwork, I examine PRR discourses and narrative strategies, and how grammars of exclusion are reconfigured across time and space. While I use online sources to analyse what themes and imaginaries are mobilized amongst populists online, the book also examines the dynamics of nationalism as expressed and embodied in everyday life. Applying content analysis alone can run the danger of methodologically reifying a static description of social life, between practice and attitude amongst one group (rendered active and immoral) against another (passive, but innocent) (Jean-Klein 2001). What is recognizable as populist nationalism in the online communications of the radical right might not exist or have relevance on the ground.

Despite the substantial and growing scholarly attention given to PRR parties, conventional theorizing tends to ignore the so-called demand side of populist nationalism: the voices and concerns of voters. While macro-studies highlight the structural conditions and motives for large segments of populations, we know less about nationalist engagements in everyday life, impeding our understanding of its dynamics and appeal. While populist nationalism can be approached from above as an ideology or discursive pattern which claims to represent and protect the purity of the imagined nation, it is made and sustained by individual agency and has to be explored and unpacked in place, in the historical, political and social context in which it occurs (Knowles 2003:48, Twine and Gallagher 2008:6, Fox 2016). Opposing the supposition that populist nationalism is only discursively produced and institutionally imposed from above (Hobsbawm and Ranger 1983), I examine how it can be embodied as an intimate form of cultural practice (Herzfeld 1997), and cognitive framework (Brubaker 1996, Lakoff 2008) that is invoked and reproduced by social actors in everyday life (Skey 2011, Fox 2016).

While some studies focus on individual support for PRR parties (e.g., Rooduijn 2014), few studies are grounded in ethnographic inquiry, thus tend to be weak in theorizing local perceptions, strategies and variations. Noteworthy exceptions are Holmes (2000), Gingrich and Banks (2006), Kalb and Halmani (2011), and Teitelbaum (2017), which all offer insights into the motives and causes of radical right nationalist engagements. The lack of face-to-face engagement with the 'real-life context' of supporters of populist nationalism is notable, but hardly surprising. Few scholars want to invest the considerable time or establish the ties necessary for the ethnographic study of people who might expose values they do not necessarily share (Blee 2007:121). However, clearly we have to understand better the motivations and concerns of supporters of PRR parties if we are to better understand the forces challenging liberal democracies.

Underpinning processes of externalization of migrants and minorities is a popular emphasis on territorially based ideas about bio-social purity, culture and 'roots' in a particular land (Müller 2016, Gullestad 2006). The study of ideas about purity and the dynamics of inclusion and exclusion link up with central anthropological questions about how the boundaries of the nation are being drawn, enlivened, and contested (Barth 1969, Douglas 2005, Pelkmans 2006).

Following Fredrik Barth's work on ethnic boundaries (1969), Brubaker (1996) suggests that we should focus on what social actors *do*, and how and when people identity themselves, perceive others, experience the world and orient their actions in national, ethnic or racialized terms. Ethnographic fieldwork, as the established approach and core of anthropology's methodological toolkit, is well suited to investigate the everyday gendered dynamics, emotional mechanisms (Blee 2007, Hochschild 2018) and taken-for-granted foundations (Fox 2016) of nationalism that tend to be overlooked in conventional theorizing.

Addressing the gap in state-of-the-art studies, I conducted six months of ethnographic fieldwork to examine the motivations and concerns of supporters of the radical right. I conducted fieldwork in towns where PRR parties have obtained a double-digit electoral breakthrough, dividing my time between Doncaster (England), Ózd, Martonvásár, Budapest (Hungary), and Oslo (Norway). In all sites I was interested in how supporters conceive their selves and belonging in an era affected by fast, accelerated change. How did registers of perceived ethno-religious or economic threats shape identification, embodiment and encounters in everyday life? How was racism and xenophobia invoked, understood and expressed by its perpetrators? What were the various motivations for engaging with anti-minority or anti-migrant discourses? How did my interlocutors' concerns align or challenge elite, political narratives? These were just some of the questions that guided my research.

Shared experiences and conversations over time are key to developing ease between informants and the researcher. As much existing scholarship has been distorted by an over-focus on men, I made an effort to include the concerns and motivations of female supporters of PRR parties. In all countries under investigation I spent time with a few key informants and their wider networks. I conducted semi-structured interviews and participant observation in multiple and changing day-to-day settings (home, workplace, public space, political meetings and social media). Fieldnotes were taken as the primary means of collecting data from observation. Another way I collected data on the nature and appeal of national populism was through recorded, semi-structured elite interviews with dozens of informants from different vantage points, such as national members of parliament and local PRR politicians and civil society actors. Finally, I observed political rallies and conferences. To ensure voluntary and informed consent of research participants, I obtained verbal consent. Besides elite informants who wanted to be identified with full names, I have assigned pseudonyms to informants for the purpose of anonymity.

The combination of qualitative data-gathering methodologies both online and offline enable the creation of a rich ethnography or, as Geertz (1973) has called it, 'thick description' of the demand and supply side of exclusionary nationalism. Moreover, combining ethnographic fieldwork with an analysis of discourses propagated by PRR parties will provide an analytical vantage point from which to observe the appeal, goals, methods and tensions of PRR actors. By combining methods we can also better understand the future directions populist nationalism might take.

The struggle over identity and recognition in overheated Europe

As the following chapters will demonstrate, processes of large-scale change since the early 1990s affected my interlocutors' socio-cultural and economic contexts with a direct impact on their personal lives. Many of the supporters of PRR parties I got to know felt excluded from the circles of power and recognition, and that they had to protect or fight for their identity status and place in society. In the fieldwork I conducted in the post-industrial town of Doncaster, material conditions were conducive to nationalist populism. However, 'overheating' in Doncaster had less to do with the economic crisis in 2008 than the past three decades of economic transition and demographic change. The lower-educated working class felt vulnerable under a new economic reality where they had to compete with Eastern European labour migrants over low-skilled jobs. In Hungary, a country hit hard by the economic crisis and affected by migratory flows in 2015, the PRR parties Fidesz and Jobbik mobilized both the economic and cultural dimensions, arguing that illegal, Muslim migrants pose a threat to jobs, culture and Christian civilization. In oil-rich Norway, where the economic crisis of 2008 was less pronounced, protectionist discourses of the governing populist Progress Party were not primarily grounded in arguments about economy, but linked to concerns about cultural integration and assimilation and dominant ideas of Norwegian-ness. Indeed, the electoral support for PRR parties in more materially secure countries like Norway, Sweden and Switzerland suggests that economic conditions alone are an unsatisfactory explanatory model.

Whatever the different factors conducive to populist nationalism, what united my interlocutors, was that nationalism became a powerful source of identity in the face of societal ruptures. The nationalism propagated by the populist radical right had local appeal because it played on both fear and actuality of cultural and economic dislocation. In England and Hungary, Ukip and Jobbik strategically targeted the populations in deprived post-industrial towns, promising a regained path to idealized notions of citizens and community. The attraction of the parties was partly due to their ability to turn traces of nostalgically remembered pasts into a model for imagined better futures. Playing upon the fears and longings of a disillusioned and dissatisfied electorate, the PRR parties promised to protect the voters against threatening forces and reinstall a sense of social security. While many of my interlocutors expressed concerns about the impact of increasing diversity and economic competition on belonging and welfare, politicians translated these grievances into an elevated politics of fear that racialized and securitized migrants in the image of a threatening other. Despite clear ideological differences between the PRR parties I have examined and the fact that the parties operate in different geographical and political contexts, all deployed dystopian imaginaries of 'crimmigrant' others (Aas 2011) to reinforce the boundaries of the nation. PRR parties were quick to capitalize on the refugee crisis to boost popular support for their already hard opposition to immigration. Migrants from Muslim-majority lands were framed as criminal intruders, as collective threats to national identity, culture and cohesion. The PRR racialized the (predominately white) constituents in deprived regions, moving them symbolically from the 'neglected and forgotten' margins of the state to the forefront of the nation in the image of its ethno-cultural defender. This appeared as a powerful formula to my interlocutors, many of whom already felt alienated from their government and a sense of being hurt by European integration and immigration.

When examining the links between economic and cultural crisis, immigration and anti-minority sentiments, it might be tempting to only do research amongst the white disenfranchised lower classes. After all, research shows that PRR voters are overrepresented amongst the male (increasingly female), (predominantly) white low-skilled lower-middle or working classes. However, only targeting working-class constituencies would be misleading. While Ukip drew most of its electorate from the older, less well-educated, white working class, the Hungarian Jobbik draws parts of its electorate from the young-generation and higher-educated urban middle class (Thorleifsson 2017). To flesh out some of the differences across countries and between supporters, I have strived to include participants of diverse age, gender, and educational and employment status.

Nationalism and anti-minority sentiments are sensitive topics to research. As an anthropologist, I set out on an open-minded quest to understand my interlocutors, rather than undermining their cause. I took their fears, grievances and concerns seriously without trivializing or denying the harmful effect of those who harboured racial or xenophobic resentment. With the exception of neo-fascists I interviewed in Hungary at a Jobbik rally, who openly embraced violence, I avoid the term extremist. As Teitelbaum (2017:7) notes, by calling nationalists extremists or deviant we might 'be declaring ourselves privy to an ultimate reality – some particular state of heterogeneity and ambiguity inherent in the human condition – of which they are ignorant'. It is equally important not to essentialize nationalists. People can be xenophobic on one occasion, and cosmopolitan on another. Still, working over time with people whose political convictions I do not share, and at times witnessing exclusionary practices was emotionally draining. While the politicians I worked with joked that they had given access to a liberal researcher, I was rarely asked to explain my own political beliefs and, as such, largely avoided situations where my interlocutors would have been offended.

The structure of the book

The analysis I am presenting in the book can be summarized as follows. The first chapter explores the local history and set of conditions conducive to the rise of populist nationalism in the post-industrial town of Doncaster affecting the UK. Based on ethnography, interviews and archival research, the chapter shows how Ukip supporters, while being negatively affected by deindustrialization, strived to cope with and give meaning to the changes affecting their lives. Examining the tensions emerging out of the intersection of various scale-making projects over meaning, memory and identity, I suggest that the rising appeal of English nationalism cannot be reduced to neoliberal restructuring, nor just the legacies of industrialism, nor to the passage of transition or global migration. It is all of these which constitute the Ukip code.

The second chapter moves from the level of everyday life amongst Ukip supporters in Doncaster to explore the populist nationalism propagated by Ukip politicians. Comparing the discourses propagated by Ukip with the Trump campaign, it shows how the figure of the non-white, (predominantly) Muslim migrant served to rejuvenate violent imaginaries of ethno-racial and religious-civilizational difference. The populist parties did not seek to reinforce national identity around a whiteness that was explicitly racially marked, but rather referred to culture grounded in (Judeo-) Christian civilization and, implicitly, whiteness as a basis of inclusion. Appeals to nationalism and cultural heritage were used to mask the extent to which anxieties over ethno-religious difference motivated reactionary politics.

The third chapter examines how the Hungarian PRR parties Fidesz and Jobbik exploited the refugee crises of 2015 to re-narrate the enemies of the Hungarian national. Following the theoretical lines of Bauman (2004), it suggests that the initial state securitization of migrants was not grounded in the logic of 'human waste'. On the contrary, it was the hyperinstrumentalization of migrants as an economic threat that prompted their further racialization and dehumanization in the image of the 'crimmigrant' Other (Aas 2011). Through the securitization of migrants from Muslim-majority lands in far-right discourse and practice, the boundaries of an imagined Hungarian nation were reconfigured and reinforced.

Chapter 4 explores the way in which violent imaginaries of Sweden have been discursively constructed and used by PRR parties in Europe. Just as the figure of the alien 'conceptual Jew' or Muslim can feature in racist imaginaries as a threatening Other (Bauman 1989, Esposito and Kalin 2011), I argue that violent imaginaries of Sweden have emerged in radical right anti-immigration discourses, practices and narrative strategies. The chapter demonstrates how individual acts of violence are 'transvaluated' into violent imaginaries of migrants from Muslim-majority lands. What I term 'the Swedish dystopia' not only entails a message of alarm and warning. PRR parties use the trope of the Swedish dystopia in their call for action against the Muslim migrants and minorities.

Chapter 5 explores populist and nationalist discourses and practices directed at the Roma minorities in Norway and beyond. It shows how the widespread association of Roma with disorder and waste is a key feature of contemporary antiziganism. In discourse and practice, Roma have been marked as a threat to the ordered and disciplined body/nation, indirectly helping to re-invent the boundaries of national identity.

The concluding chapter revisits the main themes, offering some comparative reflections on the drivers, methods and grammar of exclusion of the populist radical right.

1 From coal to Ukip

The struggle over identity in post-industrial Doncaster

Multiscalar overheating

In May 2015, the UK Independence Party (Ukip) got its breakthrough in the UK general election on an anti-immigration, anti-EU and pro-coal platform. The same month I arrived in Doncaster, a working-class town of 18,000 inhabitants, in order to examine the rise of Ukip. The party had obtained 24.1 per cent of the local vote, an increase of 20 per cent from the last general election in 2010. Over the course of three months, in May, June and September 2015, I conducted a total of 30 interviews with Ukip politicians and supporters as well as attended party events and conferences in Doncaster. Before I move on to the analysis of Ukip's affective politics of fear, it is key to examine the circumstances conducive to the appeal of populist nationalism in a traditional Labour heartland. Based on archival research, secondary literature and ethnographic fieldwork, the following explores the local history and set of conditions central to the rise of Ukip, appropriating nostalgia for 'Fordist forms of feelings of stability and belonging' (Muehlebach and Shoshan 2012) with exclusionary 'coal nationalism'.

In the mid-1980s, Doncaster, a white-majority[1] working-class town in South Yorkshire, went from boom to bust when most of the coal mines shut during Margaret Thatcher's neoliberal restructuring programme. In Britain, as a society structured heavily around class, the white working class in Doncaster typically belonged to the lower tiers of society, pushed to the margins for centuries as cheap labour in heavy industries. Doncastrians were far from the accelerated growth in London and other urban regions, experiencing a crisis-laden cooling down of the economy with rising unemployment and precarization of labour (Standing 2014). At the same time, diversification processes intensified due to increased global migration. The past three decades, Doncaster has thus been marked by a combination of social forms and ideals constructed at various scales of time and space. Taken together, the accelerated changes caused by neoliberal restructuring of the economy and global migration constitute an *overheating* effect (Eriksen 2016). One consequence of overheating is that 'different parts of societies, cultures and life-worlds change at different speeds and reproduce themselves at different rhythms' (ibid:9). Another (un)intended consequence of overheating, such as socio-economic inequality, has experienced varied growth at multiple geographical scales, from nation-states to regions and neighbourhoods (Sassen 2007).

Recognizing the multiscalar and multitemporal character of both neoliberal economic transition and diversification processes (Vertovec 2007), the following explores the multiple tensions and contradictions emerging out of processes of overheating and cooling-off in Doncaster since the early 1990s. People in Doncaster were not merely victimized by neoliberal policies, but actively strived to cope with and give meaning to the changes affecting their lives. In the space left by the dissolution of industrialism, new competing scale-making projects over meaning, memory and future played out. Some actors engaged with the town's industrial past, nostalgically appropriating coal as a source of national and regional identity. A few chose to align themselves with cosmopolitan globalism, celebrating the town's old and emerging diversity. Others embraced Ukip's anti-migration and anti-EU politics when faced with existential uncertainty. The chapter suggests that the appeal of populist nationalism cannot be reduced to neoliberal restructuring, nor just the legacies of industrialism, nor to the passage of transition or global migration. It is all of these, which in turn constitute the Ukip code.

A coal place

Several scholars have shown how long-term neoliberal restructuring of economies as well as short-term developments like the more recent financial crisis (2008) have accelerated socio-economic inequalities at various scales (Carrier and Kalb 2015). The following section examines the effect of and responses to structural change and economic transformations in Doncaster, taking the early 1980s as the point of departure. At this particular moment in time, industrialism was fundamental to British national identity. Like other towns in South Yorkshire, Doncaster was synonymous with the coal and mining industry. In an utopian mode, it was referred to as the 'Northern Jewel of England' and a site for endless progress fuelled by fossil fuels. 'Coal was king' and it was impossible to imagine a future when the bustling region would not depend on or thrive because of it. In addition to jobs in the pits, thousands worked in the National Coal Board's office and in firms that made mining equipment or provided support services to the men who went underground. Other major employers included the tractor maker Case, or International Harvester, as most people called it, and mega-factories such as Bridon Wire and Pegler that provided jobs for tens of thousands of skilled and semi-skilled manual workers.

In the mid-1980s, Doncaster went from boom to bust as a pit-closure programme went into full swing under the Thatcher Government. Thatcherism represented a programme of neoliberal restructuring, spearheading the policies that would become the dominant political and ideological form of capitalist globalization throughout the world. Faced with the declining profitability of traditional Fordist mass-production industries, states began to dismantle the basic institutional components of the post-war settlement and to mobilize a range of policies intended to extend marked discipline, competition and commodification throughout all sectors of society. Neoliberal doctrines were employed to justify the deregulation of state control over major industries, dismantling Fordist labour relations and Keynesian welfare programmes (Brenner et al. 2009).

In Doncaster, the neoliberal policy agenda had immediate and devastating effects. Several collieries shut and other major employers were 'shedding jobs like confetti'. Unemployment shot way above the national average and in pockets hit more than 40 per cent. Resistance to the closing of the mines took form in the Miner's Strike of 1984–1985 that was a terrible struggle for communities across the UK (Tuffrey 2011). The closing of the mines resulted in stagnation and deprivation, themes that were frequently covered by the local newspapers, *The Doncaster Star* and *The Doncaster Gazette*.

A survey amongst youngsters in former pit communities in Doncaster in 1993 showed that more than 40 per cent would like to move elsewhere (*The Doncaster Star* 1993). Locals were not passive victims, but active respondents to the effects of the changes. In 1997, the Coalfield Communities Campaign issued a manifesto to every member of Parliament (MP) at Westminster that said: No other industry in Britain or the rest of Europe has suffered such savage and sudden cutback. It has been an economic hammer blow. Pit closures have devastated not just miners and their families, but entire communities. But where is the help we deserve? The campaign claimed that unemployment, poverty, ill health and spiralling crime were the direct result of the pit closures (*Yorkshire Post* 1997).

The miners, albeit in a Fordist compact of management–labour collaboration, had experienced job security, fully equipped with extensive social rights and organized in trade unions. Mining was a physically demanding and risky form of work that nevertheless created visions of camaraderie that extended from the workplace and into social life. Mining, like Fordism, was in short an 'affect factory', organizing women, men and children into an 'econometrics of feelings' (Muehlebach and Shoshan 2012). When the mining-related industries closed, families did not only lose their job, but also the very activities that gave locals a sense of community, identity, certainty, dignity and friendship.

The precarization of labour

Ten years after the Miner's Strike, in 1999, the EU recognized South Yorkshire as one of the most deprived areas in Europe, sparking investment in the region's regeneration. Unlike post-industrial towns like Sheffield and Leeds that have developed strong service-sector economies, smaller industrial towns like Doncaster continued their relative decline. Despite the investment in new infrastructure, a new library, council hall, a lavish cultural centre and the Robin Hood Airport, growth was low. Unlike other towns in England such as Leeds and Sheffield that previously had relied on traditional industry for jobs,

Doncaster saw little growth during the good times (Mollona 2010). New jobs were created in sales and customer service, leisure and sales, but not enough to curb the relative deprivation of the borough.

The economic decline accelerated in the mid-2000s (Beresford 2013). One week before Christmas in 2006, more than 300 jobs were lost when McCormick Tractors closed down its Doncaster manufacturing plant after 70 years, switching production to Italy (Tuffrey 2011). If the labour conditions during the industrial era were rough and risky, the neoliberal and service-oriented economy has created even worse living conditions. According to the Office of National Statistics, Doncaster Central, a ward of around 18,000, has one of the highest youth unemployment and teenage pregnancy rates in the country, poor educational attainment, poor levels of health and pockets of high crime rates (ONS 2003). Doncaster, and particularly those relying on the enterprise economy, was hard hit by the global financial crisis that intensified the recession that had begun two decades earlier. In 2009, the glass production at Polkingson in Kirk Sandall closed after nine years of manufacturing. In 2010, more jobs were lost when the railway firm Jarvis closed and the City Council underwent restructuring. The numbers of job seekers' allowance claimants rose faster than the national average, reinforcing the relative deprivation of the town.

John, a hairdresser in his mid-fifties, has run a salon in Doncaster for 30 years. Located at the northern part of Highgate in a greyish three-storey building from the 1970s, he complained that his business was struggling. Some of the difficulties he attributed to the spatial restructuring of the town. Before, Highgate street was buzzing with life. After many shops were relocated to Frenchgate, a combined shopping centre and interchange for traffic, customers moved away from the market areas. His shop is now surrounded by boarded-up shops and one of many tattoo parlours that are located in the town. John is proud that he has managed to be in business, but described dramatic changes. Before the financial crisis of 2008, John had customers who would regularly come to have their hair coloured and cut. John noticed a sharp decrease in customers when the crisis hit in 2008:

> Women started to colour their hair at home. And you could see more on telly these commercials for home dyeing products. We had to cut staff. It became very difficult to do business here. And I cannot say it has improved. Today you see shops opening and shops closing. Like during Christmas. You had these pop-up shops selling Christmas decorations for a few weeks and then shut. You see a lot of this now.

For John, and many other struggling shop-owners, the financial recession merely exaggerated the pre-existing dynamics set in place by major economic transformation. In an age of globalization and accelerated change, places that once experienced stability have become uncertain and precarious (Bauman 1998). Labour in globalizing Doncaster had gone from being predictable, to insecure and vulnerable to marked fluctuations. The part of society recovering from its dependence on heavy industries, felt exposed and vulnerable under a new economic reality associated with casualization where they had to compete with cheap labour from elsewhere. Mining that once represented stability, now entailed highly uncertain future prospects, being vulnerable to forces beyond the reach of the community, such as the world price for coal and EU environmental policies.

In June 2015, during fieldwork, Hatfield Colliery, England's last remaining privatized deep-pit mine located in Doncaster, closed one year prematurely. The closure, resulting in the loss of some 500 jobs, brought to an end almost a century of mining. The situation that already was precarious turned into yet another defeat. The decline and marginalization of the mining communities have paralleled increased wealth concentration and growth in the metropolitan areas. The widening gap between an affluent London and deprived Doncaster can be analysed as a localized version of the Global North and the Global South divide, revealing the very logic of neoliberalism across geographical scales: its production of socio-economic inequality (Ekholm Friedman and Friedman 2008).

In addition to the restructuring of the economy, Doncaster's demographic composition has changed over the past 30 years. Doncaster, while being a white-majority town, has always been multicultural. It has the largest Roma and Traveller population in the UK. However, in the 1990s and later 2000s, diversification processes intensified due to global migration. The process has been analysed by the sociologist Steven Vertovec as 'super-diversity', or the 'diversification of diversity', reflecting more ethnicities, languages and countries of origin. Since the EU enlargement and opening of borders, the biggest rise in new residents has come from Poland and Latvia. In addition, descendants from the first waves of British Commonwealth citizens from India, Pakistan and the West Indies who migrated to the UK after World War II have relocated to Doncaster where housing is comparatively cheap. After English, Polish is the most spoken language in Doncaster Central, followed by Kurdish, Urdu and Panjabi (localstats.co.uk). Along the main street of Highgate, a large variety of cuisines reflect the different ethnic communities present in town. The names of stores and restaurants and the myriad religious congregations reflect the town's old and new diversities. Located in the centre of Doncaster is the 'Chinese, Indian and Oriental Supermarket' and 'Polskie Delikatesy' (Polish delicatessen). In the context of the UK, the diversity is not extraordinary, but locals said that these are rather new developments in Doncaster. Several 'kippers' (supporters of Ukip) I interviewed claimed that all the Polish shops were indeed indicative of how Britain had 'lost its identity'.

Nostalgia in an age of uncertainty

Turbulent times can lead to, as many scholars have noted, the proliferation of narratives about the past, the enforcement of cultural stereotypes, the rediscovery of religious identities and strengthening of ethnic nationalism. A

Figure 1.1 A Polish shop in Doncaster
(photo courtesy of the author)

typical response to radical social and economic change is nostalgia. Nostalgia can be approached as a form of social imagination that plays with the lateral possibilities and the longing for what might have been but is now unattainable because of the irreversibility of time (Pickering and Keightley 2006). Particularly, in times of existential insecurity, nostalgia can function as a potent source of social reconnection and identity (Strathern 1995).

In Doncaster, the tension between an idealized past and the discomfort with the present state of affairs surfaced as a frequent theme in the narratives of former miners, their children and grandchildren. Several of my interlocutors valued experiences and practices constitutive of individual and collective forms of self-understanding during industrialism. Transition as progress or improvement of life as promoted by Thatcherism had a counterbalance in experiences with loss of status, resources and self-worth. The promise of economic growth and prosperity at the invisible hand of Adam Smith did not materialize. Pit closures resulted in economic stagnation, and consequences such as deprivation and spiralling unemployment.

The dramatic changes remained fresh in locals' memories, even during casual chats. Lucy (49 years old), working as a receptionist at a family-owned hostel, recalled with bitterness and emotion the devastating consequences the closing of the mines had had for her family:

> We are still lying with our backs broken. My father, my uncles, cousins and brothers, they were all miners. I went down the pit with my father as a child. Mining was in their blood, and in mine. My husband Paul moved to different pits as each closed. We hoped the pits would be saved for the next generation, for our son. For Paul it was like this. He quit school on Friday and was working the pits by Monday. Like his grandfather and

Figure 1.2 A pound shop in Doncaster
(photo courtesy of the author)

father had done. People don't realize that in our community, mining was all they ever known and done.

Responding to my interest in the local working men's club, Bob (70) showed me framed black-and-white photos of Doncaster. The widowed grandfather of three is working part-time in the club that for generations has played a central part in community cohesion for the working class. Located in the Frenchgate Interchange (a £250 million structure and the 18th largest shopping centre in England), the club seemed out of place next to a selection of standardized chain stores like H&M, Tesco and Debenhams. Talking with nostalgia about the old days, Bob remembered his working life. He left school at the age of 14 and began working in a local mine. A photo depicting Rossingly colliery appeared loaded with meaning. 'It hurts, yes...', he says. Bob recalls in a low, but firm voice: 'I had my last day at the pit 7th May 1993. I remember the time, 2:40. It was a tear-jerking moment. British coal put me on the scrap heap. That was it. Who would employ a 47 year old?'

A sunny Friday in June 2015 I meet with Stewart and Jennifer Jones at Market Place, which has been the historical centre of Doncaster for centuries. Amongst fishmongers and fruit sellers, the couple in their late sixties spends time with their four-year-old granddaughter. Stewart and Jennifer, who met in their teens, returned to Doncaster from a six-year stay in Benidorm when their granddaughter was born. Their daughter and their son-in-law both have retail jobs, but cannot afford the cost of nursery. 'I'm telling you, Britain has become an absolutely terrible place to live!' Jennifer says upsettingly.

> It is a disgrace. Young, hard-working people who are struggling to pay their mortgage. Who have to use foodbanks. They can't even afford to buy their own home. And Doncaster has some of the cheapest housing in the country! Things have changed here, and I don't mean for the better.

'Born and bred' in Doncaster, Jennifer remembers her childhood with affection. Her father worked at the Railway Plant, her mother was a housewife:

> Although I was the only child, my dad never spoilt me! I wished for a bicycle, but never got one. To my confirmation I got a gorgeous cocktail watch, but he never gave me that bike. I have tried to pass that one. I would walk an extra mile to save a pound. I like Doncaster, but things are changing here. We used to have the door open, now they are all locked. I would be careful to go into town at night with all the anti-social behaviour and vandalism. Today who will take care of a neighbour that fell ill? Do you know the name of your neighbour? I love Doncaster and the community. I prefer Frenchgate to Meadowhall [shopping centre in nearby Sheffield]. But the community is rapidly disappearing. No, we won't get those days back. They are gone. If I could I would have

remained in Spain. It was this one who wanted to go back [she said accusingly, pointing the finger at her Scottish husband].

Jennifer, smoking a cigarette, laughs towards her husband. Stewart, a self-declared Scottish nationalist, proudly reveals his tattoos, including a blue-faced Mel Gibson in the role as William Wallace, the thirteenth-century Scottish warrior who fought against King Edward I of England, a bagpipe and a purple thistle. A bit later, the upbeat and smiling man looks momentarily crestfallen:

> They may have tried to take away the pride and the hope in our communities, but we're still here. But I'm glad I will not be around in 100 years' time, because there is no future here! It is just getting worse. The richer are becoming richer and the poorer are becoming poorer. Before, you knew where your job was. You could take care of your family. But all that is gone now. I pray to God that I will die before my children.

Stewart and Jennifer believed that Britain was changing for the worse. They morally evaluated the present through the lens of an idealized past (Herzfeld 1997), expressing a sense of loss and nostalgia for 'Fordist forms of feeling of stability and well-being' (Muehlebach and Shoshan 2012). Working the mines, Bob had experienced a long period of hard and dangerous labour, that also provided a sense of economic and social security. Now, in times of precarious labour, feelings of security and solidarity appeared lost or under threat. The erosion of a sense of community was a cause for feelings of estrangement and dissatisfaction. Their children's experience of great economic distress might have strengthened Jennifer's nostalgia and wish for a better life in Spain. A life outside England or even death were described as better options than witnessing the decline of the community and the uncertain future facing their children. However, more than just economic facts, Jennifer expressed an affective attachment to an era of security and modesty, values that she felt no longer existed in Doncaster. Through memory and longing for a return to Spain, she strived to cope with both a sense of structural entrapment and loss of self-worth.

Branding Doncaster into the future

The moral evaluation of the present through the lens of an idealized representation of the past can be a very practical form of action. The past three crisis-laden decades, various actors in Doncaster have appropriated the industrial era and icons to provide hope, inspiration and guidance in face of hardship and an uncertain future (Smith 1999). Since the late 1990s, many efforts to transform Doncaster into a distinctive and proud place have been heavily centred on the restoration and commemoration of its industrial past. At the early stages of economic transition, the City Council launched a campaign to attract more commerce, industries and tourists to the struggling borough, hoping that it would ease people off welfare into work. The leaflets and brochures invoked the region's coal-mining heritage, referring to Doncaster as 'England's Northern Jewel'. Rather than suggesting new routes into the future, the campaign invoked the source of historical wealth, power and energy that have shaped Doncaster. The local historiography narrated at an exhibition at the museum and art gallery at Cusworth Hall also reflects praise of the past. A poster commenting on where to go after industrial Doncaster reads as follows:

> The Railway came to Doncaster in 1849 and with it rapid industrial development. In the 19th century a wide variety of firms were established in Doncaster producing taps, planes, cars, glass, nylon, mustard, motors, plastic pipes, metal ropes, tractors, clothes and lots of sweets. This was all on top of the railway Plant works and the coal mining. Most have now gone and Doncaster faces *a new future*. But it is a future that is not so very different. The town's excellent road and rail links will still play a *vital role in what comes next*.
>
> (emphasis added)

The entire exhibition ends with a poster titled 'The Ever-Changing Face of Doncaster':

> Over the last hundred years or so, there has been a whirlwind of demolition and development in Doncaster. Development was sparked off by the coming of the coalmines. Although the speed has slowed down, development has continued. Today the town is experiencing a revival as it emerges from the trauma caused by the closure of so many coalmines. The 1960s developments are already making way for something new.

The exhibition glorifies Doncaster's industrial past without specifying what the present entails. The present is defined by the trauma of the closing of the coal mines, a loss that the local communities are shaped by. The only certain aspect of the future is that it will 'bring something new'. The vague prediction for the future is that it might not be so different due to the very transport networks that brought modernity to Doncaster. The exhibition reveals how the industrial era is nostalgically commemorated as a golden age of security, whereas the present and future are narrated as uncertain.

Connections between the industrial past and present surfaced as powerful themes in local tourism. I meet with Colin Joy, the local tourism manager. We walk a stretch of the main road Highgate and he points to various historical buildings located between rival pound shops:

> While people in Liverpool would be proud and protective of their city when they meet outsiders like you, Doncastrians would not. If you say

the town is bad they will moan in agreement. Media tend to focus on the negatives. But there is a lot to be proud of in Doncaster! The town was the home to the confectionery firm that invented butterscotch! The most famous and fastest steam locomotives like the Flying Scotsman and Mallard were all built in Doncaster. We have the remains of an original Roman wall, and one of the few Roman shields ever found. Out of the extremely few (less than ten) Roman shields ever found, one was discovered at Doncaster in 1971 and is called the 'Danum Shield', but this is not even taught in schools. When Ian Blaylock established a brewery last year, I encouraged him to call it Doncaster Brewery. If Doncaster was celebrated as much as York celebrates itself, then Doncaster would definitely be the better of the two. We need to put Doncaster back on the map!

Like the council campaign of the 1990s and the museum exhibition, the local tourism strategy is invoking, although more enthusiastically, the industrial past to turn Doncaster into a new, distinctive place its residents can be proud of. The strategy has already materialized. Two recently constructed pubs are named after the two most famous steam locomotives built in Doncaster at the Railway Plant: the Mallard and the Flying Scotsman Tap. A local group wants to re-name Doncaster Danum, the name the Roman settlers gave the area around the Don river as early as the first century AD. The settlers chose Danum as a northern outpost due to its geographical location. Situated in the centre of England along the main trading route, it was perfect for both trade and defence. Led by 'Britain's longest serving head teacher', Tony Story, the group hope that by highlighting the town's Roman roots and pioneering role in the development of the railways, they can help to soften the town's rough reputation as an anti-social hotspot.

A group of three men I interview at the working men's club described a town that had lost its 'old bubble and fizz' and turned proud when they talked about the mines. Still, they were upset with the name-changing proposal. 'You can't shake off Doncaster's reputation simply by rebranding. It would put the town on a par with Sellafield', Paul (56) says, drawing parallels to the nuclear power site which was renamed from its original Windscale after Britain's worst nuclear accident.

> You have these people who want to give Donny a trendy twenty-first-century makeover. But new names and fancy hotels won't sort out the kind of problems we have in town. The mines closed. The town has gone down and down and down. You see loads more people in the social clubs now. People who critique Donny just don't understand what it's like when the work goes. Your life just spins out of control.

After our discussion, Paul began to sing a song that was used during the Miner's Strike, resisting the pit closures. His deep, rich voice filled the room and the sincerity with which he sang brought tears to the eyes of his two friends, who soon joined in. 'They talk about statistic, about the price of coal, the price is our communities, dying on the dole.'

The nostalgic invocation of the past reflects a town that is struggling with the transition from a place where the heavy industries, the coal mines in particular, are no longer major employers. The council campaign and icons, the museum exhibition from 2005, the tourism strategy of 2015 and the embodied commemoration of a past lost can be seen as scale-making projects invoking various temporalities to reimagine Doncaster in a globalizing world. Moreover, these practices and social imaginaries resemble processes of 'structural nostalgia' (Herzfeld 1997), in which timescales and events are collapsed into generic, imagined and stylized accounts of the 'heartland' and 'the good old days' (Taggart 2004).

The temporal compressions found in memory work in Doncaster are evident in the multiple temporalities that are being invoked from the industrial era to the town's Roman roots. The industrial past is nostalgically remembered as an era signalling stability, as opposed to the uncertainty, socio-economic decline and demographic change of the present. Many of the people in Doncaster were tied to the Labour Party, through generations, the unions and their upbringing, but were still quite value and socially conservative. These voters felt alienated from the 'New Labour' that they claimed had embraced a far too progressive and socially liberal agenda.

Blaming the EU and immigrants

Perhaps the most controversial mobilization of popular nostalgia for an idealized past is that of Europe's political radical right. In many deprived European towns, a notable response to socio-economic decline and demographic change has been the heating of exclusionary identity politics and call for the reinforcement of symbolic and physical borders. In May 2015, Nigel Farage's anti-EU, tough-on-immigration populist politics won over nearly 4 million votes in the general election. Ukip got its electoral breakthrough in Doncaster, obtaining 24.1 per cent of the vote, an increase of 20 per cent from the last general election in 2010. The party became the second largest after Labour, on a heavily anti-EU, anti-immigration, pro-coal platform. Ukip tapped into the grievances of the dispossessed community, effectively addressing the post-industrial cultural, economic and racial anxieties related to fast change. Moreover, the party structured feelings about one's future drawn from a nostalgically remembered industrial and imperial past. Ukip promised to restore the past greatness of the struggling mining town. It would reinvigorate the coal industry and secure jobs in fossil fuels. It would secure the nation's border against the alleged economic and cultural threats posed by immigrants, both Eastern European and non-European migrants, they blamed for taking jobs, scrounging welfare benefits, straining health services and threatening the British way of life.

'We can't take more people!'

In the previous sections, I have examined the historical conditions and structural circumstances conducive to the rise and appeal of Ukip's populist nationalism. In May 2015 I arrived in Doncaster to examine how local Ukip supporters framed their support for the party. What were the motives, concerns and aspirations of supporters, party members and local politicians? How did registers of perceived ethno-cultural and religious threats shape identification, embodiment and encounters in everyday life?

People I met, especially those on low pay in the private sector, worried that migrant labourers from Europe had a negative effect on their living standards leading to housing shortages and wage stagnation. While a London School of Economics and Political Science (LSE) study (Wadsworth et al. 2016) shows that British workers' wages have not been hurt by EU immigration, people I met in Doncaster believed that immigrants from Poland and other Eastern European countries reduced their own limited employment opportunities. Contrary to only framing migrants and minorities as dangerous and polluting others, Ukip supporters framed newcomers as competitors in a precarious labour market, a factor driving anti-immigration sentiment. 'The immigrants are stealing our jobs' or 'We are still unemployed; we can't afford housing while the newcomers get all state benefits' were common complaints.

One of the first people I met in the town centre who expressed these views was Liz Brown, a 57-year-old woman. A lifelong Labour supporter, she has recently decided to vote for Ukip. She fits the average profile of a Ukip voter; they are predominantly over 55, white, socially conservative, suspicious of diversity, distrustful of government and politicians, and angry about perceived breakdown for authority and institutions (Stellings 2015, Goodwin and Ford 2014:157). Like many other of my interlocutors, Liz seems happy to chat about her motivations for voting Ukip. Liz was born in Doncaster and moved to Sheffield for work in a factory before returning to look after her elderly parents who had now passed. Liz was 15 when she had her son, Paul, who works at the local McDonald's. Liz hasn't had a job for 16 years.

While the heyday of Doncaster market is gone, the historical city square is still a bustling place. Liz is a regular customer at the coffee stand and greets people as they pass by. Dressed in a worn-out Planet Hollywood T-shirt, with greying hair and lacking a few teeth, she chain-smoked as we conversed, sitting on the edge of her pushchair. It is a sunny day and our conversation is occasionally broken by the excited scream of children playing and vendors shouting out their offers. High levels of unemployment, poverty and residents on benefits mean that the city square is full of people with time to chat, but little money to spend. Lighting the third cigarette with her hand slightly shaking, she points towards a cash machine at the opposite end of the street and says with a rusty voice and in contempt:

> You see, these people coming from Poland and stuff, stealing jobs and benefits. It is a shame when we have English people struggling. I even know three English men who paid £50 to change their name into a Polish name to claim benefits! Then you have all these people coming from Iraq and Pakistan. I am not blaming them. I would have done the same thing. If I lived in a place where ISIS [Islamic State in Iraq and Syria] is I would have gotten on the first plane! It isn't the individual person who is the problem. The problem is that we took too many from these places without teaching them anything. And now they claim benefits. It is a disgrace! The EU wasted money on so many things. And then there is all the British money being spent at the EU, which could have improved lives here. [Raising her voice in excitement] We need to get the hell out of the EU!

Liz blamed the immigrants from Eastern Europe for taking benefits that she believed rightfully belonged to British nationals. She even claimed that foreign benefit fraudsters forced decent English men to follow their path and take on false identities. The myth of job- and welfare-stealing migrants was a recurrent theme amongst the kippers [Ukip supporters] I met in Doncaster. Embracing the welfare chauvinism of the party, they supported policies that would reserve welfare benefits for the 'native' population.

Debbie, 63, is having a coffee and a cigarette in the town's market square with her sister Susan, 69. They complain about rapid demographic change.

> We have lived in Doncaster for more than 60 years. I have been coming to the centre since I was a little girl [putting her hand a couple of feet from the floor]. In fact, we were both born and bred in Doncaster. We hardly recognize the place. This used to be lovely town. But now? Downtown is full of shops run by people who don't speak English. It is a shame for Britain.

The youngest sister, Debbie, who has recently retired from her job in a kiosk, is clear about who she blames and what needs to be done. 'It is the immigrants, the Asians and the asylum seekers lazing around on benefits. They are getting houses and benefits before our people.' Susan, the eldest sister, dressed in a peach-coloured floral dress, lowered her voice as she said:

> I'm not a racist, it's just the numbers of new people coming here. Britain is a small island, and we can only have so many here. We are overrun. The country is full up! Why do the politicians dump them on us? To be honest, I feel a bit lost. It is not the place I used to know. We have always voted for Labour, like our families, but now we all vote Ukip.

The elderly women had experienced rapid demographic change and the consequences of economic restructuring over the past three decades. While some kippers I interviewed even considered themselves to be inclusive, these rapid changes tested the limits of community tolerance. The hostile attitudes they expressed towards new Eastern European migrants were blended with older prejudice toward people of colour. Striving to cope with the pace of change that was experienced as quite dramatic, the women nostalgically recalled a past characterized by more economic security and ethnic homogeneity. Their mourning over a lost past was translated into a diffuse form of blame directed both at migrants and conventional politicians, turning both into scapegoats for societal ills like crime and economic malaise.

The politics of English identity and nationalism

I have made an interview appointment with Ukip local politician Guy Aston (64), who stood for election in Don Valley. I walk the few miles from Doncaster town to his rust-coloured, classical brick townhouse. Located in a more up-scale part of town, the roads are tree-lined and well maintained.

It is a Tuesday afternoon, and Aston's household is all aflutter, with his wife Bernie Aston hosting a dinner for the local Ukip party leadership. The smell of chicken curry emanates from the kitchen. Loud laughter fills the room as I am greeted by Aston, who is dressed in a thick, three-piece tweed suit and pale yellow tie. Although in his home, he looks like a retired general.

'Fancy a glass of wine?' Aston says, gesturing towards the kitchen where the dinner was about to end. After a quick introduction to the local Ukip branch, we are relocating to their living room. At the same moment, Aston's daughter is coming down the stairs. Aston points at her while jokingly saying: 'This one, she is all into LGBT rights and the diversity stuff!' He mockingly highlights his political difference with his daughter. She smiles at me, slightly embarrassed and turns impatiently.

Aston has done his research. 'You're educated at the London School of Economics, it means that you're a liberal, and that means that you are trouble!' he jokes in a friendly manner. We enter the living room. A self-declared hobby historian, he has decorated the living room walls with his historical heroes, amongst them Oliver Cromwell (1599–1658) and other seventeenth-century parliamentarians. On the wall hangs the framed wording of Magna Carta, the medieval political truce that inspired protection for liberties that reads: 'No man, of what estate or condition he be, shall be put out of land, or tenement, nor taken, nor imprisoned, nor disinherited, nor put to death without being brought in answer by due process of law.'

The bookshelves are filled with military history and Aston seems particularly fond of military metaphors referring to himself as a military leader. A talkative man, Aston compares Ukip's struggle for political power and the disappointing general election results at the national level to the formation of battalions during war. With passionate enthusiasm, he parrots a few well-rehearsed lines.

> Like the British army in 1940. We sharpen up and build our forces. In the beginning you saw an almost naïve enthusiasm, but it's gonna be a long war in Donny [Doncaster] for my troops. We're like a seasoned battalion, retreated, but not defeated.

Aston talked with resignation about the general election. Like many other Ukip supporters, he felt it was a let-down in terms of the numbers of seats obtained. Ukip won 3.9 million votes but just one MP due to the first-past-the-post electoral system that prevents small parties from gaining a foothold in the House of Commons (Goodwin and Ford 2014:112–114).

Aston is a former member of the English Democrats, whose slogan was 'Not left, not right, just English' and 'putting England First'. The party proposed to establish an English Parliament, a proposition Aston continues to support. Knowing that Ukip supporters are far more likely than those of other parties to describe themselves as 'English' rather than 'British' (Goodwin and Ford 2014:120–123), I ask about the difference between the two. With excitement, Aston replies:

> I guess English these days means not being an immigrant. And being proud of that. Our local schools are swamped with people who can't speak English. As a Ukip politician I have to say I'm doing this for Britain, but I am also doing this for England. We need to wrap ourselves in the flag of St George! We have to fight for what is English. British socialists have long undermined any sense of nationalism. But people want to belong. If we can't have nationalism, what are we then besides some people living in the land? No, we need to be proud of England. We need to stand up to the champagne socialist elite in London and all their political correctness. People are tired of being bullied by the state.

Following the party line, Aston put forward the Ukip code that is playing on fear over migration and its impact on national identity and livelihoods. In Aston's view, a mythical way of British/English life, tradition and culture is threatened from the outside, whether from the cosmopolitan London elites, migrants or the EU. The UK is controlled by a corrupt and self-serving bureaucracy and incompetent officials in Brussels, factors that fuel his anti-establishment resentment.

Aston's loathing of the EU has a long history in Ukip. The party was founded back in 1993 to fight for British sovereignty against encroachments from Brussels. The founder and first leader of the Eurosceptic party, Alan Sked, stated once that: 'I became so sick of Europe after ten years and it did seem so fatuous supporting all the myths about Europe – that it was a cure-all and a great ideal for the future whereas in fact in practice it was a kind of a government of corrupt bureaucrats who are a danger to democracy' (Hodges 1997). Aston went beyond Euroscepticism to blame all migrants for rejecting English values and way of life. While he claimed that Ukip was open to 'patriots of all colour', the hegemonic nation was imagined in terms of ethnic Englishness, invoking cultural difference as a basis of racialized exclusion. The immigrants – like the national cultural space that they are said to threaten – were often imagined in racial terms.

In Doncaster, community and self-forming symbols had for generations been tied to an industrial culture. Just as the industrial era gave shape to a distinct form of habitus, whiteness was deeply embedded in the routine structures of economic and political life. In Doncaster, as in industrial England, whiteness used to represent an implicit norm around which belonging was constructed and other ethnicities judged. Whiteness was invisible, positioned as an unmarked category, natural and universal. The previous privileged invisibility of whiteness became more visible as struggles over resources, rights and recognition took place. By identifying ethno-cultural threats, the local population could reaffirm the historical status and strive for the economic security traditionally afforded to them by virtue of their whiteness. However, as I will show in the following section, not only white, working-class Doncastrians, that make up the majority of local support, were eager in their support of Ukip's strict immigration policies.

Minority support for Ukip

While some Ukip voters were whitening Englishness, fiercely excluding differentiated other from the imagined English nation, Britishness allowed more hybrid identifications. Where Englishness was emphasized as a more authentic source of identification, Britishness was used by populist nationalists to include historically minoritized Sikh others in the image of defending Christian civilization against ethno-religious threat. Several kippers could inform that they were trying to forge strategic alliances with members of the Sikh minority. The many ethnic shops and Sikh temples in Doncaster would not necessarily seem like fertile ground for anti-immigrant sentiment. At a national level, non-white voters are very unlikely to vote for the party (Stellings 2015). Yet I encountered several Doncastrians of Sikh minority background that were enthusiastic about Ukip. They framed their support in terms of competition for unskilled jobs in a precarious labour market, nostalgia for colonial Britain and fear of Islam.

A man named Aadi, in his mid-fifties, working in a local chemist, turned his own struggle for recognition into a rationale for supporting Ukip's anti-immigration politics. Dressed in a crimson turban, Aadi serves customers, wipes the counter and arranges adult magazines on the narrow shelf behind him, all while explaining his support for more restrictive immigration policies. Invoking kinship terminology to justify exclusion of new migrants, he states that:

> The house is full, and you can only have so many guests. I have worked very hard to get this job. I would wash; I took all kinds of jobs. I have served customers for 24 years. I have worked long, hard hours, seven days

a week. I look at the people from Poland and Africa who enter my shop. The people who come now are very different. Some would not have survived one week in India. You need to work and not only claim benefits. The United Kingdom used to be called Great Britain. What is it now? United States of Europe?

It might come across as paradoxical that Aadi, a British citizen who once was an immigrant, now calls for a halt on immigration. Himself a part of a minoritized group that has been subjected to racialization, social disadvantage and discrimination, Aadi believed the UK was made worse by immigrants. To Aadi, his status and socio-economic position in the imagined British home is threatened by Central and Eastern European and global immigration. He highlighted his own difficulties with adjusting to life in England and how he struggled to master English while working around the clock. Aadi had only voted once before and that was Labour. But due to what he imagined to be 'hundred of thousands' of migrants entering Britain, he voted for Ukip and would vote for Brexit (short for British exit from the EU). However, Aadi seemed to distance himself from the historical hardship he had endured by scaling globally to include an appreciation of the colonial era and the British Raj. The British Empire was like other colonial projects – inherently violent, based on the exploitation, dispossession and displacement of people across the globe. Still Ukip's nostalgic vision offered economic, religious and civilizational protectionism that also appealed to the local Sikh community. Like other locals, they were equally vulnerable to economic insecurities. If not sharing the same sense of cultural dislocation as the former white, working-class miners did, many shared the reluctance toward migration, in particular from Muslim-majority countries. Some Sikh kippers I interviewed feared that Britain was on its way to become an Islamic caliphate and that this would happen in the not-far-distant future. They used their historical memories of Islamic aggression toward Hindu and Sikh communities as a rationale for supporting Ukip. 'We need a party that can guarantee that the UK will not be overwhelmed with Muslims.'

At a Ukip conference I meet VJ, a London-born Sikh whose father arrived from East Africa in 1962 and who is one of the descendants of Commonwealth immigrants. In contrast to most of my working-class interlocutors in Doncaster, the Ukip politician from the Yorkshire branch is of a middle-class background. The 38 year old went to the same university as I did, LSE. He was an undergraduate student in Geography, but dropped out after a few months to establish his own IT business. It failed and he established his own small farm outside Yorkshire and became involved in politics. He has been a Ukip member for five years. When I ask why he became active in politics, he jokingly states: 'It is in my blood!' Turning more serious he says that part of his motivation for supporting Ukip is his concern with the recent wave of immigrants from Eastern Europe and the burden he believes it puts on the local environment and economy. VJ was clear what the appeal of the party was to voters: 'Ukip are doing well here because of the flood of Eastern Europeans in Doncaster', he said.

> I am not a racist. My grandparents and parents are Asian. But there are a lot of people coming in now. The pace is just too fast and they are too many. Immigrants can be hard workers but there is too much pressure on the system. I don't think Britain is getting many qualified migrants at the moment. Britain is losing its identity with all those Polish migrants.

While there was little space for Sikhs physically to position themselves as 'white English', they included themselves in Ukip's nationalism as proud post-colonial subjects and British patriots. Subjected to the same kind of 'othering', the Sikhs reproduce some of the colonial logic in order to exclude racialized, in particular Muslim, others. Thus the Sikhs realigned themselves with the white working class in their support for Ukip to negotiate their own position within the British imagined nation and empire. By supporting Ukip, they distanced themselves from white European labour migrants, darker migrants from Africa and, most importantly, from Muslims. The Sikh support for Ukip strengthened in turn the overall project of appealing to white Englishness and cultural difference as a basis of exclusion. The paradox is that minority supporters of Ukip reproduced the hierarchy of belonging that constitutes Britishness, while reinforcing the ethno-national logic of Englishness grounded in existential angst about England's place in the world.

Cosmopolitan Doncaster

While the industrial era is nostalgically remembered, there are social actors in Doncaster that promote alternative temporalities, allowing locals to believe that their future can be imagined according to logics that lie outside structural nostalgia for the industrial past or protectionist nationalism. Acknowledging the town's old and enveloping diversity, in May 2014, Warren Draper founded the magazine *Doncopolitan*, demonstrating a 'cosmopolitan competency' to ironize communitarian rhetoric of absolutism. According to its editorial statement, the 'magazine will big up anything which has the potential to add to Doncaster's metropolitan appeal' and counter all the moaning about Doncaster as a 'cultural desert'. The first issue of the magazine was titled *Fake it Till You Make It*, promoting themes such as diversity, the green movement, gay rights and anti-fascism. The editorial ended with the sentence 'We'll celebrate Doncaster's culture, arts, style, music, people, fashion, lifestyle, architecture and even *its coal black underbelly*' (*Doncopolitan* 2014). The editor's embrace of diversity accompanied by a somewhat joking invocation of coal reflects how the cosmopolitan is capable of inhabiting multiple worlds expressing attachment both to a valorized past and a fast-changing present. Particularly, the younger generation in Doncaster appeared less nostalgic and more prone to draw on global cultural and economic flows to assign meaning and value to their lives.

Susan (22), a student of graphic design at the local college, whom I chat to at café Culture, envisioned a Doncaster modelled around cosmopolitanism and innovation, both of which she claimed Doncaster lacked:

> There are those people looking to the past for inspiration. But those days are gone. The coal belongs to the past. As does Maggie [Thatcher]. What would we be without the EU? All our industry has moved abroad. You have these people who want to fly the Union Jack, but those days are gone. We need to listen to each other. We need more innovation, something that the town does not portray at the present. I have many ideas of how the future can look like in Doncaster. My father's friend works at the Messe Düsseldorf convention centre. Doncaster is very well connected with the Robin Hood airport. Imagine how many jobs a similar exhibition centre located next to the airport would generate! Why can't Doncaster be like Düsseldorf?

Invoking the entrepreneurial successes of a convention centre in Germany, Susan compared Doncaster's post-industrial struggling landscape to another European landscape. Moreover, in contrast to other informants supporting Ukip's call for Brexit, Susan insisted that Britain's, England's and Doncaster's economic future was intimately linked to Europe. Susan was representative of a group of voters Ukip has had far less success in appealing to; the better-off, graduates and those under 40 (Goodwin and Ford 2014:117).

Even amongst the self-identifying kippers I met in Doncaster there were clear generational tensions. Some, in particular from the older generation, felt alienated from a Labour Party that had embraced a progressive consensus. They were united by a nostalgia for the 'good old days' and the hope that a vote for Brexit would bring back the security traditionally afforded to them by the virtue of their white, English identity. The younger kippers were like the older value-conservative, but appeared much more cosmopolitan-oriented than their parents and grandparents.

Vicky Johnson (26) worked at one of many local beauty salons in Doncaster. The run-down building was located amongst shuttered shops in what had once been a vibrant place. Vicky grew up in the 1990s, when Doncaster was dealing with deindustrialization, decline and job loss. She is considering voting for Ukip, but is quick to distance herself from the racism some associated with the party.

> I don't mind the town changing. I am used to the multicultural. It's the way I know town. People have mixed together. But my grandmother for instance ... when she sees the certain types of people, for instance gypsies spending hundreds of pounds to go to the Races to see the horses run. And my grandmother – she has no money. She won't even come into the

town centre because of all the Eastern Europeans hanging around. I understand why she gets upset in a way.

Vicky pointed to the generational differences that can exist with regards to prejudice. Growing up in a more diverse and interconnected era, Vicky was eager to highlight that diversity was a normal contextual situation. At the same time she was accepting her grandmother's prejudice, empathizing with her sense of feeling threatened by migrants and minorities. The competing values and tensions between generations were indicative for many of the people I met. My older interlocutors expressed nostalgia for the industrial past and felt that migrants challenged their place in the ethnic or socio-economic hierarchy, in contrast to younger informants that tended to embrace more cosmopolitan values of being open to difference. Vicky's grandmother's motivation for supporting a hard Eurosceptic platform seemed to be a search for identity and stability in a fast-changing town. In contrast to her grandmother, who viewed migrants and minorities as threatening and disposable others, Vicky embraced diversity as an irreversible fact on the ground. Although not fully supporting all Ukip's solutions, she agreed with portions of the party's platform. She spoke with passion about the need to be proud of English heritage and the need to secure jobs in the extractive industries.

Climate denial

If Ukip framed migration as threatening to British welfare and reproduction, coal was framed as a sustainable source of energy. Ukip is in favour of reinvigorating the UK's coal industry. Roger Helmer, Ukip's spokesperson on industry and energy, is a fierce climate change denier. The former Conservative who is now a Ukip member of the European Parliament (MEP) is known for some of the most controversial remarks from Ukip members, on everything from climate change to same-sex marriage. At Ukip's annual conference in Doncaster, the party's energy spokesperson, Roger Helmer, promised 'to keep the lights on', securing jobs in the extractive industries for another 200 years. Wearing a Ukip badge, Helmer gave me a lecture in the pressroom about the 'black propaganda from the green lobby in London':

> We hate the ugly, ghastly windmills. Our enemy number one is the windmills. Our policy is to reopen the mines. We have at least enough coal reserved for 200 more years. We do not ... regard CO_2 as a pollutant. It is a natural trace gas in the atmosphere which is essential to life on Earth. Coal is a cheap and reliable energy, so why not build more coal plants? The problem now is that steelworkers in Rotherham and miners in Doncaster will lose their work due to the damning taxations and emission restrictions imposed by Brussels and London. ... For every job created in the renewable sector, four jobs are destroyed elsewhere in the economy.

While Helmer promised that the party's actions would restore jobs, he admitted that this was more 'lip service' to a topic resonating with voters than reality. 'We know that the coal mines are gone. They belong to the past. The coal mines are literally killing the people who work in them.' While Helmer admitted that the classic coal mines are not coming back, he denied that they are bad for the environment and insisted that there were ways to build clean coal plants.

The author of Ukip's official energy report, *Keeping the lights on*, conveys not just opposition to the UK's participation in the EU, but also a mixture of anti-environmentalism and disregard of scientific evidence (*Ukip Daily* 2012). Appropriating the plight of those affected by UK industrial decline, Helmer predicts an energy apocalypse at the hands of Brussels, climate scientists and wind power. He constructs the image that the British economy and cultural identity depend on extractive industries. Helmer's stance reflects how nostalgia can be applied as a powerful device in the quest for political power. A nostalgic embrace of coal as the model for the future might appeal to parts of the struggling electorate in Doncaster where coal has occupied a proud position over generations and where the numbers of jobs provided by extractive industries have been dramatically reduced. The end of coal has reinforced 'coal nationalism', where coal is turned into a key symbol of security and imagined Englishness in relation to threatening outsiders.

Conclusion

The industrial town of Doncaster was for decades emblematic of a golden industrial age. Up until the mid-1980s, the economic and cultural identity of Doncaster was connected to the mining industry that provided a sense of identity, security and future. In post-industrial Doncaster, fast, accelerated change in the form of long-term economic precarity constituted an 'overheating effect' that in turn has fuelled struggles over identity and belonging and rendered the town's meaning open to contestation. Doncastrians were not merely passive victims of changes beyond their control, but strived to cope with and give meaning to the neoliberal globalization processes in which their lives were entangled. In 2015, three decades after the privatization of the mines began, my informants' social experience was partly formulated in terms of disillusionment with the present. The transnational causes that gave them a sense of identity – Protestantism, industrialism, imperialism – are either weak or absent. In the space left by the dissolution of industrialism, combined with accelerated immigration and natural minority increase, new competing scale-making projects over meaning, recognition and belonging played out. In response to existential insecurity, some residents created a local identity around a golden industrial age, appropriating the past in various places and identity-making projects. Others invoked Doncaster's enveloping diversity, the lost British Empire, the EU or other places beyond Britain's border to cope with social and economic decline. The tensions emerging out of the intersection of the various scale-making projects in Doncaster partly constitute and make visible the struggle over identity and direction in globalizing England, between a society open to European integration and diversity and one that closes its borders on the path of rising English nationalism.

In Doncaster, the end of coal has proved consequential for the fuelling of nationalism. The interplay of the legacies of industrialism coupled with the precarization of labour and increased migration were key factors nurturing the rise of Ukip's populist nationalism. With its combination of EU hostility and emphasis on the protection of national identity and borders, Ukip increasingly appeals to the losers of globalization at the precarious edges of proper society, in particular the disillusioned working class. Ukip taps into the anxieties of the working class disillusioned with immigration, economic transition and European integration. Thriving on a fearful electorate, the party provides a future modelled around a proud history of extractive industries and protective nationalism. The promises of putting a temporary halt to all immigration and pulling out of Europe had local appeal for Doncastrians who blamed the multiple consequences of fast, accelerated change on migrants. Several of my interlocutors in Doncaster, many of whom expressed nostalgia for the industrial past, discomfort with migration and neglect by Labour, were particularly receptive to the simple answers offered by Ukip. Ukip offered a nationalist solution to existential anxieties that appealed to past privilege associated with empire and an 'indigenous', (predominately) white identity. Essentializing the less-educated working class as representing the authentic and pure 'people', Nigel Farage, a former Tory who resigned from the party during John Major's leadership, moved Doncastrians symbolically from the structural margins of the nation to its forefront in the image of its patriotic ethno-cultural defender. The populist messaging had appeal for parts of the electorate in Doncaster, who struggled to reconstitute and restore identities in post-industrial England.

Note

1 Doncaster is predominantly white working class and the 'non-white' population make up around 4.4 per cent, significantly lower than the number nationally at 12 per cent (ONS 2003).

2 In pursuit of purity

Populism and the politics of whiteness

I attend a Ukip workshop in Doncaster entitled 'training for kippers'. Around 100 members, many of them elected councillors, are gathered around round tables. Around 20 women are present but few of them raise their hands during the Q&A session. It is by all means a white and male crowd that has gathered for training on issues ranging from media and campaigning, to policy and image. The party is working intensely to professionalize the party and polish its image. A Ukip media expert encourages members not to post offensive images and refrain from using racial slurs. Openly racist friends on Facebook must be removed, in particular those from the far-right political party and anti-Muslim organization Britain First. While Britain First has failed at the ballot box, it has millions of followers online, including 1.3 million Facebook likes. Before the general election in 2015 the far-right organization was responsible for vigilante 'invasions' of mosques, distributing letters and leaflets endorsing Ukip. The group stated that 'Ukip at the ballot box and Britain First on the streets' would be a winning combination. The media trainer emphasizes that any connection to this group 'will look bad for the party' and instructed those present to cut ties, if they had any, to Britain First online as 'they are nutters and not someone who should be associated with our party'.

Ukip tried hard to disassociate themselves from far-right actors in their attempts to professionalized the party, build a more respectable public image and broaden the party's appeal. The party has been met with ridicule and outright rejection from other political parties. Back in 2006 Prime Minister David Cameron referred to Ukip as being home to 'mainly fruitcakes, loonies and closet racists'. Local protesters I met in Doncaster referred to Nigel Farage as a 'racist scumbag' and a 'disgrace for our town'.

Ukip central denied all charges of racism and was trying to professionalize the party and police boundaries to the far right. Gawain Towler is head of press, and John Gill from the London press office is a well-liked figure who has played a key part in Ukip's communications for many years. He encouraged members to have a positive engagement with the media. 'If there is a topic you don't know, make sure to repost from the national branch.' 'Talk local about local issues or pretend to be busy, call back, it gives you time to think.' 'Never post something when you are angry or under the influence of alcohol.'

As I will show in the following, attempts to mainstream the party appeared alongside calls to withdraw into particularism and promote the uniqueness of a distinct people, a process Teitelbaum (2017) terms the new nationalist double imperative. While PRR parties did not seek to reinforce national identity around a whiteness that was explicitly racially marked, the arguments about the need to protect 'our cultural heritage and Christian civilization' reinforced whiteness as a basis of inclusion. Examining the supply side of populist nationalism through discourses propagated by Ukip and the Trump presidential campaign, I suggest that the figure of the non-white, (predominantly) Muslim migrant served to rejuvenate violent imaginaries of ethno-racial and religious-civilizational difference. Racialized, anti-immigration discourses and practices claimed the protection of bio-social purity, serving to re-territorialize (predominately) white identities.

Trump's use of racism

Nigel Farage's associate across the Atlantic, the American President Donald Trump, apparently did not know about Ukip's training session in Doncaster. If far-right ideologues used to be confined to the margins of the internet, then Trump embraced the Islamophobes. On 29 November 2017, President Donald Trump retweeted three inflammatory videos by Jayda Fransen, the deputy leader of Britain First. Trump is not the only politician who has spread Islamophobic propaganda. Terje Søviknes, the current minister of petroleum and energy from the Norwegian Progress Party, retweeted videos from Britain First in March 2017. When confronted with the source of the material he apologized and said he should have checked closer and not used a feed by Britain First. Donald Trump, however, did not apologize for re-tweeting fascists until being asked to do so by the conservative British journalist Piers Morgan, one of only 45 people the president follows.

Trump's use of racism to gain votes was evident during the 2016 presidential campaign. Breitbart News editors, like Milo Yiannopoulos, pushed white ethno-nationalism as a response to so-called political correctness. The comment section became a thriving arena for white supremacist meme-makers which saw Trump as a champion of the idea that America is fundamentally a white man's country. During the campaign, former Ku Klux Klan leader David Duke repeatedly stressed his support for Trump's candidacy, saying: 'I'm overjoyed to see Donald Trump and most Americans embrace most of the issues that I've championed for years.' Trump himself was slow to distance himself from Duke and his particular racial interpretation of the 'American Dream'.

The white nationalism mobilized in the Trump campaign must be understood in the context of history. The US was historically a racial settler state where the white population identified itself as the legitimate 'people'. For radical nationalists, ranging from the neo-fascist to the identitarian, the electoral slogan of the Trump campaign – 'Make America great again' – implicitly seeks to restore values associated with white masculinity. Trump has confirmed this assumption with racist political actions after being elected president. He has banned citizens of chosen Muslim-majority countries from entering the US, marking an entire cultural-religious group as posing a security threat. Trump has retweeted white supremacist messages, including one that falsely claimed that black people were responsible for 80 per cent of the murders of whites. Trump was also slow in condemning the violence committed by white supremacists at a rally in Charlottesville where a white supremacist rammed his car into a crowd of counter-protesters, killing one woman and injuring at least 19 others. Trump's highlighting of violence on 'both sides', producing a moral equivalence between neo-Nazis and counter-protesters, emboldened these groups further. David Duke, in a video at the rally, said that: 'We're going to fulfil the promises of Donald Trump. That's what we believed in. That's why we voted for Donald Trump, because he said he's going *to take our country back*, and that's what we got to do.'

'I am not a racist'

In contrast to Trump's overt racism and reluctant condemnation of white supremacists, kippers I interviewed would often utter the phrase, 'I am not a racist, but ...' Indeed, many kippers were keenly aware of the charges of racism associated with Ukip and were trying to demonstrate otherwise. A common strategy that would render charges of biological racism difficult to sustain was to refer to non-white members of the party. In general I found that there was a significant preoccupation with skin colour, as the following ethnographic examples will show.

In May 2015, I visited the Ukip campaign office in East Laith Gate, in Doncaster. The office, heavily decorated with voting leaflets and nativist posters, is located between the Shabir Indian Restaurant and Spices kebab takeaway. A male local politician I meet proudly said that the man living across the street was 'black and a kipper'. At a party event, the same politician introduced me to Steven Woolfe, a mixed-ethnicity former barrister who grew up in a working-class neighbourhood in Manchester, as a sign of the party's inclusive character. An older, male politician who wanted to remain anonymous said:

> I am not a racist. We *kippers* believe in traditional values. You have people like Russell Brand corrupting young people. And you have migrants not behaving. Like in Rotherham. But the political correct elites accuses us of racism. We must break out of the burka called political correctness and the multicultural indoctrination. This is not about colour, it is about behaviour. Ukip is open to patriots of all colours.

Roger Helmer, Ukip's spokesperson on industry and energy, expressed similar explicit references to skin colour. The former Conservative who is now a Ukip MEP is known for some of the most controversial remarks from Ukip members, on everything from climate change to same-sex marriage. Wearing a party badge and wide-stripe tie in the Ukip colours, Helmer introduced himself by handing me his business card containing a photo of himself and two of his female assistants. 'You see, they are both brown-skinned. Of Indian and Caribbean decent. So you see, there are black people in Ukip as well. The white faces you will see at the Labour meetings. Not a black or Indian face will appear there! It is absolutely nonsense that we are racists!' It appeared as if Ukip politicians of minority background were valued as members in their role in re-branding the party as non-racist to increase the likelihood of electability.

Ukip defines itself as a 'civic' nationalist party and rejects biological 'blood and soil' racism. Following the party platform, several of my interviewees emphasized the party's alleged inclusive character and openness to anyone who wishes to identify with Britain, regardless of ethnic and religious background. While rejecting the old type of racism based on ideas of inferiority and superiority between racial groups, several of my interlocutors would exclude those seen as cultural outsiders. This 'new racism' (Barker 1981) does not 'construct an explicit racial hierarchy but rather an immutable fixed and organic belonging of specific people, territories, and states that in effect excludes and racializes all "Others"' (May et al. 2004:224). While whiteness was not always located on the body, it was imagined as an investment in a system of values and practices that associated Englishness with whiteness. Processes of racializing others tend to occur around perceived social problems, such as immigration and crime, that become associated with people marked as 'dangerous others' such as migrants, Muslims, people of colour, Jews, Roma or other minorities. The following sections will illustrate how processes of racialization were practised by Ukip and the party's Leave campaign (for the EU membership referendum).

Out of the EU and into the world

It is Ukip's annual party conference in September 2015. For the second year in a row, the event is located in Doncaster, at St Leger Racecourse. Although there were some local protests over the party's return, Doncastrians were largely welcoming. According to a poll by the *Doncaster Free Press*, 76 per cent of the readers where overwhelmingly in favour of the national event being held in Doncaster for a second year. The view was largely confirmed when I spoke with Doncastrians. Danny, a small-business owner I met at Frenchgate shopping centre, hoped that the event would 'help put Doncaster on the map'. Local Ukip politician Guy Aston, whom I interviewed at his home in June, remembered the last year's conference as 'electric' as the party's leader Nigel Farage launched his 'purple revolution'. 'Farage is a straight talker. He is an amazing speaker. A real genius', he noted admiringly.

In September 2015, the ritualized political performance was repeated when the party conference was yet again held at the St Leger Racecourse, symbolically moving Doncaster from a stigmatized periphery to the foreground of national politics. The Ukip leadership has planned to further appeal to the struggling electorate, promising to challenge Ed Miliband, leader of the Labour Party, whom they claim is 'no voice for the working man'. The previous year, Nigel Farage had stated that he would 'put the tanks on Labour's lawn!' Holding the conference in Doncaster was a direct challenge to Miliband, whose constituency was Doncaster North. Ukip strategically tapped into the sense of disillusionment amongst voters who felt neglected by Labour. However, it was not obvious how their economic policies would benefit those who felt left behind as they ran on support for privatizing public services, cutting taxes for the rich and attacking workers' rights. The strategy seemed nevertheless to work. Ukip secured more than 28,000 votes in Doncaster in the general election of 2015, finishing second in both Doncaster Central and Doncaster North and third in Don Valley (Burke 2016).

Two purple-coloured vans are parked outside the venue situated within ten minutes' walking distance from the city centre. Crosses of St George and Union Jack flags are adorning nearby buildings. Flags and flowers in the Ukip colours of purple and yellow are displayed outside the entrance. Cars are decorated with window stickers saying, 'I reject EU citizenship'. Ukip teddy bears, stickers, rosettes, knitting patterns, woolly jumpers and anti-EU slush drinks are amongst the many items for sale. A female fan reveals a big tattoo of Nigel Farage on her upper arm, embracing the party leader as a real-life hero. In the reception area, hundreds of suit-wearing delegates from across the country are registering. Before the conference I received an e-mail from John Gill saying that I've been accredited as a guest/observer, as the usual category journalist would not suit my profile. With a silver VIP pass around my wrist, I am allowed full access to the venue. Journalists and researchers, although often framed in populist discourses as part of the elite, enemy establishment, are at the same time instrumental in processes of mainstreaming.

To massive applause, Nigel Farage enters the conference stage to the 1986 single by the Swedish rock band Europe, 'The Final Countdown', a soundtrack chosen to reflect the message of the conference titled 'Out of the EU and into the world'.

As a populist entertainer, Farage nurtures images of an independent, strong and prosperous UK outside of the EU, a radical alternative to the 'champagne socialist' political elites in Brussels and London that have forgotten the interests of 'ordinary' people. Farage presented a series of unavoidable terrifying futures that awaited Britons if they remained in the EU. In contrast, a bright future would face Britain if its citizens decided to leave the 'dictatorial EU project' with its freedom of labour and movement rules ,and 'take back control of the borders'. EU was framed as the external enemy, responsible for uncontrolled migration that in turn threatens jobs, exhausts public benefits

Figure 2.1 'Out of the EU and into the world'
(photo courtesy of the author)

and challenges the British and English way of life. On immigration, Ukip would put a five-year moratorium on immigration for unskilled workers and introduce an Australian points system for skilled migrants, regardless of nationality. All EU freedom of movement would end. Farage said he would stop people coming in if they have 'life-threatening diseases or criminal records'.

Not surprisingly, the central theme at the Ukip conference 2015 was migration. Since I embarked on fieldwork in May 2015, the influx of asylum seekers to Europe had reached an unprecedented level with some 885,000 migrants arriving – over five times the number in 2014. In populist discourse, the accelerated mass migration was presented as a 'wave' of illegal introducers that were threatening the nation and Christian Europe. Several of the talks at the Ukip conference consisted of scaremongering on the issue of the allegedly uncontrolled continuing arrival of non-indigenous people to the UK. Non-racial categories such as crime were mobilized to exploit racial anxieties without using an explicitly racial discourse. In an inflammatory speech, Ukip's defence spokesman Mike Hookem screened a video depicting himself riding along with an English truck driver. The driver from a working-class background feels intimidated by non-European migrants in the encampment Calais nicknamed the 'jungle'. Accompanied by action-filled music, Hookem climbs the fence to the Eurotunnel – the direct undersea route between Britain and France – to illustrate how easy it is for migrants to make it to the UK. Walking along the French–British border fence, Hookem talks about the criminal and aggressive behaviour of migrants in the region. The video ends with an appeal to exclusionary nationalism. 'Now is the time to reject the dictatorial EU project that threatens our heritage, our traditions and our way of life' (Ukip 2015).

For Ukip, the 'refugee crisis' functioned as a critical event through which violent imaginaries of ethno-religious difference were mobilized. Hookem embodied and voiced a utopian Britishness and Englishness set against the alien 'crimmigrant' other. The video framed migrants as a monolithic mass threatening to contaminate the nation, while the white working class was essentialized as a homogenous, suffering group in need of protection. While it is a fact that migrants try to get into lorries to get transported to the UK, Hookem presented the practice as an existential threat to Britain. Hookem's narrative entailed a form of 'double racializing' of the white working class, and non-white migrants. All refugees and migrants were framed as illegal aliens, only driven by economic factors and not forced to seek protection.

The Breitbart advisers

Ukip, a party protesting European integration, appears strikingly transnational when it comes to forming alliances with other Eurosceptic political actors. At the conference gala dinner, I am placed at the head table with Nigel Farage. Amongst the ten people seated around the oval-shaped table are an MP from the Sweden Democrats (SD), a former MP from the Geert Wilders-led Dutch Party for Freedom (PVV) and the Danish former leader of the Norwegian no to the EU movement. Farage is tremendously popular, and the guests attending the dinner seem to compete for his stories and attention. Farage rocks with laughter as he loudly jokes with the tombola caller.

I leave the venue with the younger delegates and share a taxi with Raheem Kassam, the 28-year-old chief adviser to Farage. He introduces me to his female friend who works for the Trump campaign in California. She is attending the conference to get inspiration and input that can be used in the American presidential election. A Trump campaigner at the Ukip conference in Doncaster demonstrates the close political cooperation across the Atlantic. Kassam was headhunted by Stephen Bannon, co-founder of Breitbart News, to run Breitbart's London office. Like Bannon did for Trump, Kassam temporarily left his Breitbart position to become the chief adviser to Farage, referring to him almost 'like a father figure'. Bannon and Kassam advised their respective candidates to focus on the threat from 'illegal aliens' and radical Islam.[1]

Kassam told me that although the best way to communicate was to knock on doors and distribute leaflets, Ukip was being boosted by a natural movement of 'cyber-kippers' spreading the word online. Social media, Twitter and Breitbart in particular were instrumental in mobilizing support for the party. Kassam advised Farage to stick to a radical agenda and be tough on migration. While the Trump and Brexit campaigns were cultivated in different geographical and political contexts, the essentializing of the white working class and stoking of fears for 'crimmigrants' were similar. Several of the dystopian themes used by Ukip and the Leave campaign were evident in the presidential campaign of Donald Trump, who referred to his victory as 'Brexit, plus, plus, plus'. Donald Trump's run for office electrified radical right actors. When Kassam's head-hunter Bannon embraced Trump, Breitbart was turned into the website of the so-called 'alt-right', essentially a rebranding of white nationalism meant to make it appear more acceptable in the political mainstream.

During the American presidential campaign, Stephen Bannon 'embodied' the defiant populism at the core of Trump's agenda. According to Bannon, the nation is threatened by progressive, liberal elites. The American dream of progress and prosperity has eroded in a country on its way away from God and towards the brink of societal collapse. Trump's inaugural speech was remarkably dystopian and bore Bannon's stamp. The speech entailed a series of themes that played upon the hardships of an essentialized American working class in the rust belt. Trump spoke about factories as tombstones and promised to stop 'the American carnage'. In a populist tone the enemies of the nation were invoked. The scapegoats for various societal ills were the politically correct elites and the corrupt Washington establishment. In this dark world, Bannon has long praised his idols who reveal the truth. Republican Tea Party women like former vice presidential candidate Sarah Palin and Michele Bachmann, represent the authentic voice of the 'silent majority'. They stand up for 'the ordinary men and women' who feel estranged and forgotten in a globalizing US. Bannon's background as a businessman, marine officer and media editor informed his solution to America's alleged decay. Bannon is promoting economic protectionism before free trade, strongman unilateral action before slow diplomacy, and Breitbart News before *The New York Times*. Bannon's economic nationalism can be summed up in the slogan 'America first'. A new and responsible capitalism must be anchored in Christian values. Bannon has quoted Lenin when he claimed that a new political order can only be created through the destruction of the old. 'The swamp must be drained' and the establishment destroyed before a strengthened nation can surface.

42 *In pursuit of purity*

The Bannon and Kassam influence on rhetoric and themes emerging throughout the campaigns were evident. According to Bannon and Kassam, the US and UK are already in a global war – against radical Islam that poses an existential threat to Christian, Western civilization. Both the Trump and Brexit campaigns effectively nurtured violent imaginaries of hordes of foreigners that would overrun the US and Europe, among them ISIS terrorists. The implicit production of white nationalism was also evident in the many non-white migrants and minorities Trump marked as enemies of the nation. Trump ran for president calling for a temporary ban on Muslims. In a dystopian discourse, he vilified Mexicans as drug dealers and rapists, invoking the image of vulnerable white women attacked by men of colour. At rallies, he invited on stage white mothers of children killed by undocumented migrants. The Trump campaign referred to Syrian refugees as 'poisonous skittles' and marked all Muslims as potential security threats.

Islamophobic fears

Like the Ukip 2015 conference, the Brexit campaign was dominated by the topic of migration. In particular, transnational, violent imaginaries of Muslim migrants were utilized in race-making discursive work. The series of sexual assaults against women in Cologne on New Year's Eve[2] committed by men of Arab appearance led to intensified anti-migrant rhetoric. German authorities stated that three of 58 suspects arrested in connection with the crimes were asylum seekers from Iraq or Syria.[3] However, PRR parties and other far-right parties and movements exploited the event to gain support for their anti-immigration views. Gábor Vona, chairman of the Hungarian radical right Jobbik party, for example, pondered over whether the Western media muteness on the sexual abuses perpetuated by migrants in Cologne is a result of a 'central decision' or 'self-censorship'; either way, it is a 'tragic' phenomenon, Vona concluded.[4]

In a discourse conflating displacement with crime, the hashtag #rapefugee started trending on Twitter. Vigilante groups emerged online vowing to protect 'our women' from the 'rapefugees'. In an interview with the far-right and conspiratorial Breitbart News, Nigel Farage cultivated a similar image of Middle Eastern migrant men as a security threat to Britain and Western civilization.

> The shocking scenes in Cologne are not far removed from us here in the United Kingdom. Whilst these men may not have EU passports, they soon will. They will then be free to come to the street of Britain. Ultimately, this whole question of border controls, identity and security are issues on which the referendum will be determined. We are at a crossroads as a country and a continent. For the good of our people and our nation we must leave the European Union and start standing up for our Judeo-Christian heritage.
>
> (Breitbart website, 8 January 2016)

In pursuit of purity 43

> **UK Independence Party (UKIP)**
> 8 January at 16:34
>
> "It is clear that the West as a whole lacks cultural confidence. Quite frankly I'm tired of speeches from David Cameron and Theresa May who seek to assert values but do nothing. We get words but very little action.
>
> "The shocking scenes in Cologne are not far removed from us here in the United Kingdom. Whilst these men may not have EU passports, they soon will. They will then be free to come to the streets of Britain.
>
> "Ultimately this whole question of border controls, identity and security are issues on which the referendum will be determined. We are at a crossroads as a country and a continent. For the good of our people and our nation, we must leave the European Union and start standing up for our Judeo-Christian heritage."
>
> Do you agree with UKIP Leader Nigel Farage?

Figure 2.2 'Pan-European Migrant Rape Story'
(screenshot of Ukip Facebook page by the author)

Farage narrated the Cologne event as if it happened 'naturally' and the United Kingdom, ordinary Britons and indeed the entire Judeo-Christian heritage were framed as the potential next victims of violent 'crimmigrants'. In the not-too-distant future, these Muslim men would be living in Britain, allowed to enter by the well-paid and politically correct leaders of the EU. Invoking an exaggerated worst-case scenario and playing upon styles of emotion already in circulation, Farage nurtured Western Orientalist fantasies about the threatening 'hypermasculinity' of male, dark-skinned foreign men that threatened white women. This was a script that Farage knew well, as Ukip had already exploited for political aim actual crimes committed by British citizens of minority background. In Rotherham, Labour administrations were critiqued for not confronting properly child sexual grooming by gangs of mainly Pakistani origin. Farage blamed this alleged failure on the politically correct establishment.

The politicization of events in Cologne and Rotherham show how crimes committed by a few in one context rapidly can be framed by the radical right and reinterpreted by a global audience as part of a wider cultural, ethno-religious and intercivilizational conflict. Such racialized and gendered imaginaries claiming that the alleged innate 'hypermasculinity' of non-white men poses a threat to the safety of 'our' women is an old colonial fantasy and strategy historically used to justify incarceration, segregation and racial profiling.

A few days before the nationwide referendum on the UK's membership of the EU, Farage exploited similar older, gendered, racial anxieties to turn fears into votes. An anti-immigration propaganda poster depicted a queue of

Syrian refugees accompanied with the title 'Breaking Point: the EU has failed us all' and the caption 'We must break free of the EU and take back control of our borders'. The picture of displaced Syrians crossing from Croatia to Slovenia was far removed from the UK. Still, the images of migrants were structured according to a similar nativist logic of a pure, static and innocent nation and civilization in danger of being flooded with Muslim migrants.

The continuation of violent imaginaries of the perceived menace of Middle Eastern enemies is fuelled by a global flow of ideas concerning notions of a clash of civilizations between the 'civilized' (Western, Judeo-Christian) and 'non-civilized' (Muslim) world. This polarizing frame of interpretation has been salient since the colonial era and has gained strength and traction in the post 9/11 era. Ukip under the leadership of Nigel Farage has indeed presented itself as the saviour of an endangered nation, standing up to stop immigration and defend the Judeo-Christian heritage (Odone 2013). The populist projection of the violent 'crimmigrant' male other makes implicitly Judeo-Christian masculinity more desirable. Similarly, white lawfulness and morals are reinforced in relation to the allegedly innate criminal nature of the male Other. By nurturing violent imaginaries of 'crimmigrants', of Muslim rape and violence, the PRR created a unifying, imagined whiteness. Moreover, mobilization of violent imaginaries of 'crimmigrant' others served to reinforce the ethno-nationalist boundaries of the nation while strengthening the image of Brexit as the solution to the endangered Western, (Judeo-) Christian civilization.

The Ukip-led Brexit campaign resonated with parts of the electorate. On Thursday, 23 June 2016, the people of the UK voted for withdrawal from the EU in a nationwide referendum, with large protest votes from deprived working-class areas. The Leave campaign saw huge support in Doncaster with 69 per cent supporting Brexit. The referendum reflected a UK divided by education, region and class. Scots, and to a lesser extent Welsh and Irish, show a disposition to pull out of the United Kingdom and make their own arrangements with Brussels. In England, it was not only disenfranchised, older, less-educated middle- and working-class whites from troubled industrial areas that opted to leave the EU; so did more affluent, social conservative southerners (Goodwin and Heath 2016). Still, at the Leave celebrations, Nigel Farage communicated to the core of working-class voters, declaring in a populist tone 'a new dawn and victory for the ordinary people'.

Framing Brexit as a victory for ordinary people's fight against the establishment was a theme that resonated with Trump's presidential campaign. At a Trump rally in Jackson, Mississippi, 90 days prior to the election, Nigel Farage made an appearance speaking about the similarities of the Brexit movement and Trump's candidacy (Ganucheau 2016). To a cheering crowd he stated that he would not vote for Hillary Clinton if he was paid to do so. Trump, using the rally to ally himself with Farage, used similar grammars of exclusion as the Brexit campaign, representing himself as the champion of 'the silent majority' against the 'establishment' of both the Democrats and

Republicans. After Trump's presidential election victory on 9 November 2016, Trump tweeted: 'The forgotten man and women will never be forgotten again.' Farage's embrace of Trump was rewarded symbolically. In 2016, he became the first British politician to meet with Trump since he was elected president, ruffling the feathers of the establishment politicians they both claim to loathe.

Conclusion

This chapter has explored how populist nationalists in the UK and US reimagined the boundaries of the nation in relation to internal and external 'others'. While Ukip supporters in Doncaster expressed concern over the impact of rapid diversification processes on culture, religion and economy, the Ukip leadership elevated these grievances through a politics of fear that reinforced a sense of threat posed to the nation. While Ukip was committed to a civic, and not ethnic form of nationalism, party politicians drew upon older, colonial, racialized discursive traditions in their framing of differentiated others. In particular, the Muslim 'crimmigrant' embodied racialized fantasies about violent threats to national identity and security. In contrast to Ukip that strives to distance the party from far-right, vigilante groups like Britain First, Trump retweeted their messages. In the US, radical nationalists and far-right extremists alike have embraced Trump as the saviour of the white race and they feel emboldened by his passive condemnation for white supremacists.

The non-white migrant appeared as a convenient scapegoat for both the Trump and the Leave campaigns. In a discourse conflating displacement with crime, the 'conceptual' forced migrant was identified as a threat to white cohesiveness, the dilution of national purity and enemies of an idealized Christian civilization. Both the Trump and Ukip Brexit campaigns entailed a strategy of dual essentialization. The 'forgotten and ordinary' white working class was racialized in the image of the authentic people, whereas non-white others were racialized as threats to national security, cultural heritage, Christian civilization and implicitly whiteness. The electoral campaigns addressed the economic conditions and cultural anxieties associated with the post-industrial experience and globalization, while racializing these into xenophobic, violent imaginaries of others.

While white nationalism was more salient in the Trump campaign, both the Ukip Brexit campaign and the 2016 US presidential campaign promoted the superiority of whiteness through discursive representations of Muslim migration. The PRR parties appealed to nationalism, religion and civilization to portray racialized migrants as strangers, criminals, undesirables, cultural outsiders. While the Trump and Farage campaigns represented two distinct forms of populist nationalism, their processes of racialization of difference followed similar patterns. This was made evident with the 'refugee crisis', when both parties appealed to nativist nationalism and (Judeo-)Christian civilization in their quest to reinforce the symbolic and actual boundaries of the (white) nation-state. Amongst Ukip politicians and supporters whiteness was implicitly evoked through 'Englishness' and the need to protect 'our culture' from the Muslim threat. Although older biological notions of race did not surface during interviews, Englishness was invoked as a racialized form of cultural belonging, which did not allow any hybridized identifications. Britishness was a more inclusive category of belonging, allowing a Sikh minority to enter a political alliance with Ukip to reaffirm their identities, thus reproducing the racialized logic of the UK nation-building project, including the imperial past. The heavily gendered campaigns designated the category of illegal male migrant as an enemy to unite their supporters. By nurturing transnational, violent imaginaries of 'crimmigrants', of Muslim rape and violence, the populist radical right created a unifying, imagined whiteness. Collective, (Judeo-)Christian identities were affirmed by marking the Muslim Other as undesirable and disposable. Moreover, the Muslim Other became a spectacular projection that met the populist needs of whiteness and Englishness, of whiteness and Americanness.

Notes

1 Nigel Farage, Raheem Kassam and members of the Leave campaign were invited to Trump Tower before Prime Minister Theresa May, and posed in front of a golden door. At the Conservative Political Action Committee in February 2017, Farage spoke alongside Bannon.
2 'Cologne police said Monday that there had been 553 criminal complaints stemming from that night, about 40% of which relate to sexual assaults' (http://edition.cnn.com/2016/01/12/europe/germany-cologne-migrants-tensions/).
3 Caroline Mortimer (2016) 'Cologne: Three out of 58 men arrested over mass sex attack on New Year's Eve were refugees from Syria or Iraq.'
4 http://derecske.jobbik.hu/hirek/vona_a_polgari_magyarorszagot_mar_nem_a_fidesz_kepviseli

3 Disposable strangers
Far-right securitization of migration in Hungary

Zygmunt Bauman (2004) reflects in *Wasted Lives*, how refugees, asylum seekers, migrants and not least *sans papiers*, undocumented migrants, can be conceptualized as *human waste* – the outcome of modernity. Wasted humans in a globalized era are the excessively overflowing, the superfluous or redundant, considered of little use and value to modern society. Presumably having nothing to offer in economic terms, there is no cure for being considered human waste by nation-states (Bauman 2004: 56). While Bauman's concept is powerful, it says less about the various ways in which people are made into waste. Bodies made disposable operate along racial, gendered and economic lines. Humans are not a priori human waste. They *become* expandable and disposable by concepts and state practices of dehumanization (Butler and Athanasiou 2013).

The examination of populist nationalism in association with the so-called 'refugee crisis' is relevant not only for understanding the exclusion from European territory of forced migrants deemed undesirable or disturbing to the nation-state, but also as it reveals some of the ways in which the homogenous perception of nationhood based on ethno-religious and cultural values (Feischmidt and Hervik 2015:3) is being re-narrated (Bhabha 1990), re-imagined (Anderson 1991) and re-invented (Hobsbawm and Ranger 1983). This chapter examines the state discourses and perceptions of the Hungarian radical right in relation to non-European (mostly Muslim) migrant Others. Based on multi-sited fieldwork in 2015, it argues that the mass influx of migrants from Muslim-majority lands was exploited by the governing PRR party Fidesz and the right-wing extremist party Jobbik to re-narrate the enemies of the Hungarian nation. Xenophobic imaginaries questioning the very humanity of migrants emerged in the far right's grammar of exclusion. Migrants were marked in practice and discourse as polluting others, posing a threat to national culture, welfare, security and even Christian civilization as a whole. The initial framing of migrants was not grounded in the logic of human waste. On the contrary it was the hyperinstrumentalization of migrants as an economic threat that prompted their further racialization and dehumanization in the image of the 'crimmigrant' Other (Aas 2011). Through the securitization of migrants from Muslim-majority lands in far-right discourse and practice, the boundaries of an imagined Hungarian nation were reconfigured and reinforced.

Purity and danger in overheated Europe

In the analysis of far-right securitization of migrants it can be productive to superimpose Mary Douglas's analysis of 'dirt' on the categorization of *human waste* as posing an anomaly to the quest for utopian purity, unity and order by the sovereign nation-state. In her seminal book *Purity and Danger*, Mary Douglas (2005 [1966]) proposes that conceptual boundaries are symbolic expressions and materialization of fundamental division in social structures. Dirt and 'dirtiness' can be seen more generally as an aberration of the system, the categories of people that are deemed threatening and conceived as 'matters out of place' (Douglas 2005 [1966]). However, an important conceptual distinction between dirt and waste, is that the world of waste might provide fluidities, mobilities and redefinitions that the world of dirt subjected to a frozen classificatory hierarchy may not (Visvanathan 2014).

The border-crossing elements can potentially be powerful or dangerous, as they both defy the lines of order and can thus be considered impure or polluting (Douglas 2005 [1966]). The border-crossing act, while filled with risk and danger, can at the same time be a zone of creative potential for change. Drawing on the work on Hannah Arendt, Giorgio Agamben (2005) notes how it is ultimately the nation-state that has the right to demarcate the border between inside and outside, citizen and non-citizen, and to police this border in the name of security of the nation-state. Agamben notes how the rupture resulting from the crossing of a border by the refugee brings to light 'for an instant' the constructed relationship between man and citizen and thus the relationship between sovereignty and bare life (Agamben 2005:131).

The local context will necessarily inform how forced migrants crossing borders are perceived and interpreted by states, societies and individuals as polluting *human waste* or as potential value that can be recycled and included in a new social body. In a Europe struggling to cope with the interrelated crises of economy and governance the crisis of protracted displacement has triggered contradictory political responses. Countries like Germany and Sweden have opened their borders to a large number of asylum seekers[1] while several Eastern European countries have categorically closed their borders to migrants in the name of state security. The crisis of cooperation is hardly surprising. European immigration policy is grounded in a patchwork of 28 hugely varying national systems constrained by national politics and shaped by culture and history. Nevertheless, the diversity of policy responses and the intensity of emotion surrounding the 'refugee crisis' has made clear the deepening polarization of contemporary European politics.

Hundreds of thousands of refugees have risked their lives to cross the Mediterranean to reach the shores of Europe. One of the multiple and complex causes of the increase is the protracted conflicts in the Middle East, North Africa and Central Asia. Particularly the brutal war in Syria since 2011 has led to the large-scale displacement of the population.[2] Across European contexts in turn, PRR parties have exploited the humanitarian crisis to reinforce anti-Muslim and anti-immigration rhetoric and policy, and are experiencing an unprecedented surge in support.[3] As the displacement in Europe stretches out in time and resembles a permanent state of exception, the societal humanitarian engagement and rhetoric have somewhat faded from national agendas and been accompanied by more hostile discourses that inflame xenophobia. Xenophobia connotes a broader set of negative attitudes or emotions directed at individuals or groups because of their perceived membership in a defined category. In particular Islam and Muslims have emerged as objects of aversion, fear and hostility in contemporary liberal democracies. Islamophobia, the rejection of Islam, Muslim groups and Muslim individuals on the basis of prejudice and stereotypes, may contain both emotional, cognitive, evaluative as well as action-oriented elements (e.g. discrimination, violence) (Stolz 2005:548).

While Islamophobia has been a well-documented phenomenon in liberal democracies in Western Europe the past decade (Mudde 2009, Berezin 2009), Islam has been less relevant to national populism in East Central Europe, except in parts of the Balkans with long-settled Muslim populations (Brubaker 2017:18). The refugee crisis of 2015 led to the growing traction of Islamophobia in the Eastern European context. In Poland, the ruling Law and Justice Party (PiS) stepped up its anti-Islam rhetoric ahead of the national elections, as did the ruling Smer-SD party in Slovakia under the leadership of Prime Minister Robert Fico.

The support for PRR parties portraying migrants as unilateral threats to 'our way of life' cannot be reduced to one single factor, but must be understood in relation to multiple causes such as neoliberal restructuring of the economy, previous experiences with diversity and immigration, the socio-economic make-up of a particular region and community, historical events and the salience of exclusionary ethno-nationalism. Taken together, these factors and processes of change constitute an overheating effect, out of which an unintended outcome is heating of exclusionary identity politics (Eriksen 2016).

The following examines the dynamics of far-right securitization of forced migration from Muslim-majority lands in the Hungarian context. In contrast to Britain and the US, Hungary was already governed by PRR parties as the refugee crisis unfolded, influencing the state and societal responses.

Framing migrants as threatening Others

In 2015, 170,000 migrants, the majority forced migrants from Syria, Iraq and Afghanistan, used Hungary as a transit country, as the first entry point for the Balkans migration route into EU countries. While Hungary received the highest number of migrants per capita in all European countries, the state categorically rejected the Franco-German quota proposal, forcing countries to take an obligatory number of forced migrants. Although the migrants had no intention to stay in Hungary and were on their way to other Western European destinations, the large-scale migration was utilized for political purposes. Still, the category of the non-European migrants was heavily securitized by the governing parties Fidesz and Jobbik as an existential threat to the Hungarian nation. Numerous state-propagated campaigns drew sharp boundaries around an imagined virtuous and pure Hungarian nation in relation to the 'lenient elites' in Brussels and Muslim 'illegal' migrants.

Present-day securitization of migration in Hungary must be analysed in relation to the ongoing battle for political power between the governing Fidesz – Christian Democrats and the country's second largest party, far-right Jobbik (Movement for a better Hungary).[4] The Fidesz party grew out of the anti-communist movement and was considered a fairly conventional conservative party around the turn of the century. Since the leader of the ruling Fidesz, Prime Minister Viktor Orbán's return to office in 2010, he has, partly under pressure from Jobbik, an extreme radical right party founded in 2003, drawn Hungary in the direction of an illiberal state, imposing an intensely nationalistic style of politics (Kornai 2015). Orbán has openly embraced ethnic nationalism and the illiberal state, thus challenging the core norms and values of both liberal democracy and the EU. To bolster popular support, Orbán has passed policies traditionally associated with the radical right and ultra-nationalist party Jobbik. Orbán has used his party's historic two-thirds majority in parliament to pass bills that effectively attack or dismantle the checks and balances of democracy: the electoral process, media and academic freedom, civil society and judicial independence. In tandem with consolidating power, Orbán has hyped up his role as Hungary's and Europe's strongman and patriotic defender of the Christian West that he claims is endangered by liberal 'globalists' such as Chancellor Angela Merkel and her support for liberal asylum policies.

While promoting similar irredentist impulses, Orbán is keen to distance Fidesz from Jobbik, their main challenger in the national elections in 2018, a party known for its antiziganism, antisemitism and racism (Wodak 2015). Jobbik's initial success was largely based on its ability to tap into widespread fear of the Roma minority in the Hungarian countryside. Presenting Hungary as a defenceless martyr of history, Jobbik's manifesto advocates strong irredentist and nativist policies and the protection of Hungarian ethnicity, welfare and identity (Jobbik 2010:11, 14–15, 19). The party rejects liberal democracy and embraces, like Orbán, the illiberal state. With over one of five Hungarians voting for the party in the general elections of 2015, it has shown critics that it is more than a one-hit wonder.

The worst refugee crisis in Europe since the Second World War brought the Muslim migrant to Fidesz as a convenient stranger at hand (Kovács 2012). Orbán could shift public attention from Hungary's scandals of corruption, to the ground of immigration and national security (Hann 2015). Contrary to Bauman's argument of forced migrants being deprived of economic value, it was the migrants' presumed threatening economic agency to precarious Hungarian jobs and livelihoods that initially was highlighted as a central theme in the state-sponsored anti-immigration campaign. Eight months before the suffering of refugees from war-torn countries such as Syria, Afghanistan and Iraq was broadcast to a global audience, Orbán launched a massive 'awareness campaign' on the alleged threats posed by migrants. The governing populist parties took advantage of the atrocity in Paris to push their own agenda. In January 2015, shortly after the *Charlie Hebdo* massacre, the government displayed anti-immigration billboards across Hungary reading, 'We shall not allow economic migrants to jeopardize the jobs and livelihoods of Hungarians', and 'If you come to Hungary, respect our culture'.

The blue billboards with white letters were written in Hungarian, thus clearly targeting Hungarian citizens only. Scapegoating migrants as threats to the national economy and culture, the anti-immigration narrative played on fear and welfare chauvinism. By referring to the urgent need to protect Hungarian economy and culture, a boundary was drawn in relation to the migrants allegedly polluting cultural practices, making them unlikely to adapt to Hungarian society. The framing of forced migrants as unilateral economic and cultural threats to the Hungarian nation was paradoxical. The overwhelming majority of forced migrants had no intention to stay in Hungary, but were on their way to other destinations in Western Europe, and Germany in particular where Chancellor Angela Merkel had unilaterally lifted the Dublin Convention for Syrian refugees. However, the narration of migrants as threats to Hungarian reproduction and well-being was instrumental for the next phase and element of the anti-immigration campaign that securitized migrants in the image of the 'crimmigrant' Other (Aas 2011).

Rendering migrants as human waste

In May 2015, the state-propagated scaremongering continued with a 'public consultation on immigration and terrorism', a 12-question survey send by mail to 8 million citizens over 18 year of age (the total population of Hungary is 10 million). The title itself associated forced displacement with Islamic radicalism and violence. In a populist discourse the EU and 'elites in Brussels' were narrated as dysfunctional and directly responsible for the crisis endangering Hungary. A terrible future was awaiting Hungary if they did not act against EU 'lenient policies'.

In a discourse, conflating forced displacement with terrorism, the consultation entailed 12 leading questions, amongst them: 'We hear different views on increasing levels of terrorism. How relevant do you think the spread of terrorism (the bloodshed in France, the shocking acts of ISIS) is to your own life?' Other questions blamed Brussels for their 'lenient policy' and 'mismanagement of the immigrant question', implying that the refugee crisis could not be solved within the existing European legal framework (Prime Minister's Office 2015a).

The economic theme of the campaign remained as reflected in the question: 'Do you agree that economic migrants jeopardize the jobs and livelihoods of Hungarians?' However, the economic threatening agency was further linked to Hungarian reproduction as expressed in the final question: 'Do you agree with the Hungarian government that support should be focused more on Hungarian families and the children they can have, rather than on immigration?' Contrasting migration with the capability of Hungarian families to reproduce further deepened the imagery of migrants as a unilateral threat to the Hungarian nation. The state-sponsored politics of fear went beyond a focus on nationalism to include warnings of the civilizational threat from Islam (Brubaker 2017).

Through numerous speeches, Orbán confirmed Hungary's belonging to the Christian West and the imagined European community of values and tradition. In a parliamentary speech on 21 September 2015, Orbán stated that it is Hungary's historic and moral obligation to protect the borders of Hungary that in turn is also protecting Europe. Summarizing his position on the refugee crisis to enthusiastic applause, Orbán said that 'migrants are now not just knocking on our door, but breaking it down. Our borders are in danger, our way of life based on respect of law is in danger, and Hungary and the whole of Europe is in danger' (Prime Minister's Office 2015b). Hyping up his role as a strongman, Orbán depicted outsiders as threatening others while representing himself as the righteous voice of the people and sole protector of the Hungarian nation and Western, Christian civilization (Mudde 2007).

The xenophobic campaign reflected populist nationalism as it drew sharp discursive boundaries around an imagined virtuous Hungarian nation in relation to the Brussels elite and (cr)immigrant others. Campaign narrating migrants from Muslim-majority lands as threats to Hungary's culture, reproduction and security, was grounded in the logic of a nation and civilization in danger. Such moral panic and hostility towards the migrant Muslim 'Other' is fuelled by a global flow of ideas concerning the 'War on Terror' and notions of a clash of civilizations between the 'civilized' (Western, Judeo-Christian) and 'non-civilized' (Muslim) world, a polarizing frame of interpretation that has been invoked in the national politics of multiple countries since 11 September 2001 (Huntington 1996).

From the Hungarian state's perspective, migrants were framed as figures of radical difference. In an apocalyptic discourse conflating displacement with international terrorism, the migrants were portrayed with certain inherent features seen as posing an existential threat to the Hungarians. The migrants were not portrayed as victims of a humanitarian emergency in search of protection, but as 'crimmigrant' carriers of dystopia – of crime, chaos and ethno-religious pollution. As dystopic threats endangering the nation, the state legitimized their exclusion from Hungarian territory.

Orbán passed, with the support of Jobbik, anti-immigration measures and policies, including the construction of an $80 million razor wire along the country's border with Serbia. The passage to thousands of refugees waiting on the other side was effectively shot down. Border crossings were criminalized with potentially several years in prison and the introduction of a state of emergency allowed the army to use rubber bullets and tear gas against refugees. The anti-immigration campaign justified the criminalization of migrants as illegal. The campaign essentialized all migrants as threats to the nation, allowing any space for individual biographies or agency. The rendering of migrants as human waste had significant consequences for those detained and treated as 'illegals'.

In Hungary, however, Orbán's politics of fear and policies enjoyed support domestically, with Fidesz rising in the polls and set to win the elections in 2018.[5] The anti-immigration campaign also functioned to nurture pre-existing xenophobic tendencies in Hungary. A poll by research institute Median in the autumn of 2015 showed that 50 per cent of Hungarians are fearful of the alleged Islamification of Europe, with 70 per cent of Fidesz voters and 63 per cent of Jobbik voters believing that sooner or later the Muslims will become a majority in Europe. Orbán exploited a humanitarian emergency to boost political support and presented himself as the strongman and saviour of Europe and Christian civilization.

Changing grammars of exclusion

The Fidesz xenophobic campaign had unintended consequences, with Jobbik making a U-turn on its traditional positive stance on Islam. This is in contrast to most Western European countries where the use of xenophobic discourse on Muslims is integral to populist politics. Anxieties about a potential or ongoing Muslim invasion have long pervaded the far-right racial imagination in Europe. Over the last decade, most violent attacks directed at Jews, first and foremost in France and Belgium, have been carried out by disenfranchised young radical Islamists who in their religiously founded identity politics conflate Jews with Israel. France's Front National, while having deep antisemitic roots, tends to focus on the growing Muslim threat and at times even declares itself as pro-Jewish. In contrast to far-right parties in Western Europe that largely support Israel and focus on the threat from radical Islam, Jobbik support antisemitic and anti-Zionist policies, the Palestinians and Iran. Jobbik politicians frequently deploy anti-Israeli, pro-Palestinian and pro-Iran rhetoric.

Jobbik is a party that traditionally has combined the 'old type' of scapegoating the Jew by linking them to modernity and internationalism with the 'new antisemitism' that holds Jews responsible for developments in the Israeli–Palestinian conflict or the political situation in the Middle East. Party leader Gábor Vona has long expressed admiration for Islam and the Muslim and Arab world. 'Jobbik has always been sympathetic to the Palestinian cause', the party states on its website. Like Jobbik MP Márton Gyöngyösi, Vona has given multiple speeches at pro-Palestinian rallies. Wearing the black-and-white *kaffiyeh*, a neck scarf, they have compared their struggle for a better Hungary with the Palestinian freedom struggle. Vona has attended a youth conference in Yemen and Gyöngyösi partly grew up in the Middle East. In his book titled *Born on 20 August*, Vona writes that 'Islam is the light to fight the darkness of globalization', and praises the religion's spiritual qualities (Vona 2012). Vona further writes that:

> I declare that today the mankind's last remaining bastions of traditional culture – experiencing the transcendent in everyday life – is the Islamic world. I say this as a Roman Catholic man. Its success or failure, in the relation of the Islam and America/Israel is not as important for me as from the aspect of mankind. If Islam fails the lights will completely go out. There will be no foeman against the darkness of globalism. Then the history will really come to an end and there will be no happy end.[6]

The absence of any sizeable Muslim population in Hungary and lack of experience with immigration from Muslim-majority lands, might explain why the main defining Others of Jobbik traditionally have been the Roma minority and Jews (Kovács 2012).[7] The myth of Roma as transnational, itinerant figures acts as a mediator of the global and the national, a quality it shares with Jews (Hutchings 2012:14).

In a discourse that would be unacceptable to most populist parties in Western Europe, Jobbik's antisemitic rhetoric is explicit, referring to 'Jewish capital', calling its opponents puppets of 'Jewish conspiracy' and invoking conspiracy theories about 'American-Jewish' plans to control the world. Márton Gyöngyösi, a Jobbik MP, said in 2012 that all government officials of Jewish origin should be officially listed as they posed a potential 'national security risk'. While Jews and Zionists are demonized by Jobbik, Roma have traditionally been the main defining other of Jobbik. Antiziganistic propaganda was one of the main causes of Jobbik's breakthrough in 2010, when the party obtained 17 per cent of the vote in the parliamentary elections (Biró-Nagy and Róna 2013).

With radical views on the Roma minority, Jobbik strategy has been to target peripheral, rural regions with large Gypsy minorities (Jobbik 2010:11). The strategy worked, and the party won narrowly in the northern industrial town of Ózd, a small town in north-eastern Hungary near the border with Slovakia, which has a large Roma population. I visited Ózd to examine the local conditions for Jobbik's electoral breakthrough and found striking parallels to Doncaster. Just as the English post-industrial town once was valorized as England's northern jewel, Ózd was once considered the proud jewel in the industrial crown of communist Hungary. A huge steel plant and iron works employed thousands. By the mid-1990s most of the industrial workers had been laid off. The unemployment rate jumped to 40 per cent and unskilled Roma were among the most affected. Today the town is governed by the 28-year-old Jobbik Mayor Dávid Janiczak who rose quickly through the Jobbik ranks. Describing himself as the 'Wizard of Ózd', he received 64 per cent of the vote, partly through politics targeting the local Roma population.

Figure 3.1 An old steel factory in Ózd
(photo courtesy of the author)

Jobbik's manifesto as well as their party magazine *Barikád*, frequently mention problems with 'Gypsy crime'. Jobbik and other far-right actors have effectively mainstreamed the fantasy image of 'Gypsy crime', stereotyping the Roma as criminal by nature and welfare-dependent (Feischmidt and Hervik 2015:6, Vidra and Fox 2014:52). The Muslim migrant as criminal thus resonates with an established grammar of exclusion in Hungary.

With the refugee crisis, Jobbik made a U-turn on its view on Islam. Gábor Vona's open praise of Islam stands in sharp contradiction to the anti-Muslim racism that is heavily present in the online campaigns, newsletters and internet debates of Jobbik. Anti-refugee sentiments are abundant on the racist website kuruck.info. One commentator writes: 'Wipe the cult Islam and Muslim followers from the face of the earth. It is time to put a little German rule into law and burn every last one of these pig loving hordes in the ovens, open up the camps again and fry the bastards.'

In the October 2015 issue of the party magazine *Barikád*, in addition to the usual invocation of a Zionist plot that threatens the Hungarian nation, migrants from Muslim lands are associated with terrorism. In line with Fidesz's populist conflation of migrants with security threats, Gábor Vona wrote on his Facebook page the same month that: 'We must prevent the quota because we cannot know who are refugees, immigrants or terrorists.' While Jobbik politicians traditionally have praised nation-states where Islam is the dominant religion, Islam is considered a threat once it crosses the border in the figure of the non-European (mostly Muslim) Other.

The migrant as pollutant

While providing political support and legitimacy to the Fidesz-orchestrated anti-immigration campaign, Jobbik simultaneously launched several campaigns serving to ignite fears and present the far-right party as the solution to the crisis. A Jobbik propaganda video posted on YouTube praises the success of László Toroczkai, the mayor of Ásotthalom, a town with a population of around 4,200, close to the Hungarian–Serbian border, in strengthening border security. The video, subtitled in English, is aiming at propagating Hungary's 'well-functioning' border control to an international audience. In a low-budget video full of action-adventure aesthetics, the mayor, walking along the razor-wire fence with a German shepherd dog, warns the migrants that coming through Hungary will be 'a bad choice' (Helms 2015). The propaganda video reinforces notions of the male protector, volunteering to ensure control and protect Europe from chaos and a Muslim 'invasion'.

The only close-up image of a migrant is of a bearded man. The phenotypical difference is constructed as a security threat, playing on popular fear of Muslim religious extremists. The propaganda video serves as a warning that Hungary is exposed to the threat or actuality of being polluted by Islam and unclean bodies. The materiality of 'waste' is a central trope of exclusion, informing the call for increased border control. Otherness is mediated in environmental terms, providing a bird's-eye view footage of waste, such as plastic bottles, boxes and old blankets, left by the migrants. The coping strategies of the migrants are presented as a cultural incapability of respecting the Hungarian wastelands in the border region. The filth, disorder and crime ascribed to the migrants are juxtaposed with the 'clean' Hungarian values and the restoration of order as promised by the radical right. The binary of poor, rural Hungarians and dirty strangers reinforces an ideal about Hungary's identity and representation. Littering, attached to disgust and morally inferior behaviour, justifies rejection of otherness while asserting the radical right's self-assessment as the civilized and righteous protector of European borderlands.

Antisemitism and Islamophobia fuse

The xenophobic campaigns seemed to influence attitudes. During my conversations and personal interviews with Jobbik members, it did not take long before fears of Muslim migrants surfaced. My interlocutors frequently pondered when the next wave of migration from the Middle East would hit Hungary. The abstract Muslim appeared as a thinking category through which violent imaginaries of radical difference were projected. A 36-year-old carpenter, who had brought his wife and five-year-old daughter to a forum on migration in the village of Martonvásár, had never encountered Muslim refugees. Still, he was passionately convinced that they were 'the biological weapon of the American and Israeli Jews who wanted to spread Islam to Europe'.

During interviews with Jobbik supporters, conspiratorial thinking of George Soros with antisemitic overtones surfaced frequently. In their narratives, the American Jewish billionaire of Hungarian descent personifies the elitist, cosmopolitans in favour of open borders that in turn threaten Hungarian identity, welfare and security. Several informants claimed Soros was a 'serial national traitor' and 'billionaire speculator'. Informants frequently spoke about his wealth and power. Gabor, my interpreter in the former steel town of Ózd, put it this way: 'George Soros, the Hungarian Jew, he took the family money. Sold the company. And George Soros stole the money.' Others insisted that Soros and a liberal, Jewish elite engulfing the globe were financing a secret masterplan to turn white, Christian Europe into a brown and Muslim caliphate. A 56-year-old Jobbik supporter held similar conspiratorial and antisemitic views. The man, who had been forcefully displaced to the Norwegian town of Sandnes in Rogaland county post-1956, blamed the migration on Jews. Moreover, he claimed that George Soros was financing a plan for the Muslim takeover of Hungary. Others again claimed that Soros used the Syrian refugees as a biological weapon to spread Islam to Europe. Such conspiratorial thinking about powerful Jews who plot the country's downfall by using Muslims as a biological weapon show how antisemitism and Islamophobia are fused together and serve as symbolic and rhetorical resources in the emergence of new grammars of exclusion (Mastnak 2002, Benbassa and Attias 2004). While the fear and fantasy relate to Jews and migrants of Muslim origin, they resemble older conspiracy theories targeting the Roma minorities. The Roma as the 'Jew's biological weapon against Hungarians' is an established conspiracy theory that is regularly invoked on the antisemitic news portal racist far-right kuruc.info (after the Kuruc, anti-Habsburg rebels of the seventeenth century) which has explicit connections to Jobbik.[8] The salience of 'Muslim migrants as the American Israeli Jews' biological weapon' thus shows how older grammars of exclusion inform the production of new racialized fantasies and fears. Jobbik's rise has led Fidesz to portray itself as a defender of national interest, which also includes a similar mobilization around antisemitic tropes and rhetoric. Pushing for illiberal policies and anti-EU reforms, billboards and full-page media ads that have appeared across Hungary depict a smiling Soros with the caption: 'Don't let Soros have the last laugh.'

Ahead of the parliamentary elections in April 2018, both Fidesz and Jobbik had been using Soros's name in their populist rhetoric. Across the country Fidesz posters appeared with the letters 'Stop Soros', warning that Americans want to settle migrants from the Middle East and Africa in Hungary and that 'the opposition would dismantle the border barrier together'. Launched in February, Fidesz billboards portrayed opposition leaders Bernadett Szél (Politics Can Be Different), Ferenc Gyurcsány (Democratic Coalition), Gábor Vona (Jobbik) and Gergely Karácsony (Dialogue for Hungary) holding wire-cutters in George Soros's embrace.

The tropes invoked in the election campaign resonate with familiar conspiracy theories circulating amongst far-right groups in Hungary and beyond, that George Soros is financing a plan for the Muslim takeover of Europe. Soros, a long supporter of democratic transition in Central and Eastern Europe, is demonized in traditionally antisemitic terms – a dangerous globalist who is destroying traditional society, security and sovereignty through his support for open border policies. Orbán's and Jobbik's antisemitic and Islamophobic imaginaries of Soros are shared by many PRR parties in Europe and the US which have attacked Soros for his support of open borders and alleged 'Islamization'. While images of the Muslim and Jewish 'other' have co-existed in Western racist thought throughout centuries, the so-called 'refugee crisis' functioned as a critical event that allowed far-right actors to fuse antisemitism and Islamophobia in new grammars of exclusion.

Insecurity and precariousness

Protectionist discourses on migrants as threatening Others are not just symbolic, but also linked to power and access to resources and uncertainty in terms of Hungary's political-economic position in Europe. Orbán's fearmongering of migrants as economic threats was so effective because the economic anxieties percolating in Hungarian society are real. The financial crisis of

2008 hit Hungary hard and the country entered a severe recession. Hungary's gross domestic product (GDP) growth rate experienced a collapse in 2009 with a recession of 6.3 per cent, compared with 3.9 per cent growth in 2006 and just below 2 per cent in 2013 (Eurostat 2014). The crisis impacted the life of ordinary Hungarians, in particular for the working class at the precarious edge of society, suggesting it might be one of the driving causes of voters move to the radical right.

In post-communist Hungary, the part of society recovering from its dependence on heavy industries feels particularly vulnerable to economic recession. Hungarians I interviewed in the post-industrial villages of Ózd and Martonvásár expressed a deep sense of economic uncertainty. While Hungary has been an EU member country since 1 May 2004 and a Schengen Area member since 21 December 2007, many felt that the progress and prosperity they were promised from European integration did not materialize.

Contrary to only framing migrants as dangerous, others that threatened to unsettle cultural space, my interlocutors framed them as potential competitors in a precarious labour market, a factor driving anti-immigration sentiment. 'We can't allow migrants into Hungary. Look how we are struggling. Even we are waiting to go abroad to find jobs. It will be impossible to integrate the migrants', were common complaints amongst people who felt that migrants threatened their own, limited economic chances. People's objective economic condition seemed less important in fostering resentment than how they were faring compared to expectations. These concerns were very similar to the ones raised by my informants in Doncaster. Although the British and Hungarian contexts differ in terms of history and demographic make-up, the racialized grammars of exclusion invoked in political campaigns as well as the concerns among their supporters were quite similar. Like Ukip, Jobbik strategically located forums on migration in deprived working-class towns, deliberately courting those who feel marginalized in Hungarian society. Jobbik has targeted the rural areas since 2003, focusing on the negative outcomes of globalization. Arguing for a new Eco-Social National Economy, Jobbik frequently make calls for the need to protect national landscapes and secure the economy of marginalized, rural communities. In addition to activities on the ground, Jobbik has the largest online presence of all political parties in Hungary, with its Facebook page boasting over 490,000 Facebook likes.

During the migrant crisis, Jobbik social media campaigns exploited local anxieties of losing one's rightful place, both in Europe and in Hungarian society. In one photo posted on Jobbik's Facebook page, a young Hungarian boy is pictured wearing a worn-out T-shirt. The accompanying text states that 'also Hungarians are poor', invoking the plight of the rural poor in the deprived countryside that are burdened with the garbage left behind by migrants on their way to wealthier countries in Western Europe. The binary of poor, rural Hungarians overrun by 'illegal aliens' can appeal to those people who are at the sharp edge of economic austerity and fearful of the effects of accelerated change on their livelihoods and way of life. Inflaming local fears, the party offered a 'nationalist solution' to existential precariousness, turning the migrant into a convenient scapegoat for societal ills. The economic arguments of the anti-immigration campaign appeal to those people who are at the sharp edge of economic austerity, justifying securitization and exclusion of migrants. Contrary to Bauman's rather static conceptualization of forced migrants as 'human waste' deprived of value, it is precisely the conceived threatening economic agency of the migrants that facilitates a space for the further criminalization of that agency, reducing to bare life those detained as 'illegal aliens'.

Although the economic arguments of the anti-immigration campaign play on real fear of being outcompeted at home, it would be misleading to state that the Hungarian radical right solely attracts voters from the white disenfranchised lower classes affected by neoliberal transformation. Jobbik, while drawing the majority of its voters from deprived areas, is also receiving votes from the young, educated, urban middle class. The anti-immigration campaigns of Fidesz and Jobbik combined three major themes – economy, culture and security – thus catering to multiple audiences, from those fearing labour competition to those fearing cultural contamination.

Imagining enemies

In October 2015, when I conducted fieldwork, the inflow of migrants to Hungary had ceased, yet at the same time the anti-immigration campaigns were in force. After interviewing numerous Jobbik members of the Hungarian parliament, I attended a Jobbik event where I managed to get deeper access to the party.

It is a rainy and windy October evening. Jobbik is arranging a forum on migration in Haller Street. I'm running to catch the event on time, having spent the preceding hour in the Holocaust museum located a few blocks up, to catch the meeting that starts at six. The door is covered in frosted glass, with the map of Greater Hungary imprinted. A soft light filters through the logo. The white-painted room of around 40 square metres is heavily decorated with nationalist symbols. A flag in red-white-green tricolour and a hole in the middle, commemorating the 1956 uprising against communism, is placed next to the entrance door. Jobbik's flags are attached ahead on the opposing wall. The Jobbik logo is an adaptation of the Hungarian flag that has been warped from the centre to form a circle onto which a white Christian cross taken from the Hungarian coat of arms has been superimposed. Earlier adopters of the Arpad stripes were Hungary's Arrow Cross, Hitler's most reliable partner. Like other radical nationalist parties and movements in Europe, Jobbik appropriates symbols, myths and terminology of a fascist past in the iconic representation of self and others. In addition to old symbols used by the interwar fascists, Jobbik uses pagan symbols like the Turul bird, a symbolic creature that figures in ancient Hungarian mythology, intended to invoke a pre-Christian, ethnically pure Hungarian past. The ultra-nationalist politicians have looked backwards and restored the past in their creative fusing of symbols. Such symbols expose a particular vision of the nation and invent historical continuity between the past and the present.

Indoors, around 20 Jobbik members and supporters have gathered. I count nine women and 11 men. While it is evident that Jobbik has managed to target the Hungarian youth, the supporters present are predominantly middle aged. A few people have gathered at the back of the room, serving themselves from a fruit platter while paging through *Barikád*, the party magazine that has a monthly circulation of over 10,000. The front page depicts a military vehicle wrapped in international newspaper, from the German papers *Süddeutsche Zeitung* and *Frankfurter Allgemeine*, to *The New York Times* and the *Daily Mirror*, firing at a map of Hungary attached to a shooting target. The headline reads 'The Line of Fire', followed by the lines 'an internationally coordinated campaign going on against Hungary', reflecting the perception that Hungary is under attack by the international community.

For a political party that depicts liberalism and multiculturalism as key enemies and emphasizes links to the East, it is keenly aware of the Western response to the illiberal turn in Hungary. There has been widespread international condemnation of Hungary's harsh response to the refugee crisis, rejecting the quota proposal as well as erecting fences along the country's border with Serbia and Slovenia. Jobbik's vice president has even hired a German-speaking assistant to read and translate the coverage of the migration crisis by German press.

A huge banner with the most high-profile photogenic young Jobbik politicians is strung across the front wall. I have met two of them already. Georgina Bernáth gave me a guided tour of the Hungarian parliament, admiringly commenting how the GR grand structure was 'built for a grand nation'. On the poster and also a speaker at the event is Dóra Dúró, a Jobbik MP and leader of the cultural committee in parliament. Her husband is Előd Novák, a previous vice president of Jobbik and one of the party's must outspoken antisemites. The party leader, Gábor Vona, is smiling to the left. The old black vest emblem of the paramilitary group Magyar Gárda, the now forbidden paramilitary group he founded, is replaced with a shirt. Like with other far-right parties across Europe, Jobbik has strived to rebrand to appeal to a wider electorate. The campaign of youthful politicians smiling and dressed in strong colours is aimed at softening their image. In the three elections in 2014 – parliamentary, European and municipal – it toned down its rhetoric and softened its image, all in an attempt to appeal to middle-class voters ready to abandon Fidesz. I met Vona a few days earlier, at the Jobbik office in the Hungarian parliament. He was sucking on a lollipop. I can't help but think that these politicians, all born in the late 1970s and 1980s, are my generation.

I sit down on a wooden chair in the middle of the room. Dóra Dúró and Dániel Kárpát, the vice president, who is leading Jobbik's underground campaign on migration, enter the room. I'm handed a Jobbik pen and paper to air my opinions in an anonymous survey that will be conducted later. Dániel Kárpát begins his speech. He stresses the need to re-establish the border guard and to operate closed camps for illegal migrants in towns and villages. In Jobbik's view multiculturalism is threatening to destroy national identity. When faced with the threat of terrorism, unemployment, migration and crime, Orbán will eventually act as 'cowardly' as all the other 'parties of the twentieth century'. It is clear that Jobbik has started to position itself ahead of the elections in 2018. Leaders I interview claim that their enemy number one is liberal democracy. They don't want to end democracy, but improve it. They offer no concrete alternative to contemporary democracy, just vague promises of making the government less corrupt, more efficient and responsive. A woman in her mid-twenties airs her fears about the dangers posed by Islam. 'They come with their Koran, and I mean, I find it scary. That they will live in our communities.' After a one-hour lengthy speech about the status of Hungary's response and the need to secure the land, the anonymous questions are read. 'What about George Soros? Is he the reason for it all?' Dániel Kárpát, half laughing, does not reply. After the meeting, the Jobbik supporter, a suit-dressed businessman in his sixties, approaches me and reveals eagerly in perfect English that he posed the question about George Soros. 'You see the Jews are the ones responsible.'

Bauman (1989:3) notes that antisemitism can exist without Jews. Along similar lines I noted a peculiar form of Islamophobia without Muslims. Many of the Jobbik supporters I interviewed lived in places far removed from the refugee routes, but were deeply fearful of Islam.

Searching for 'crimmigrants'

The following ethnographic vignette demonstrates how the Jobbik leader securitized forced migrants as a threat to the nation while inflaming xenophobia. I followed Jobbik's vice president and deputy leader of the party's Parliamentary Group, 36-year-old Dániel Kárpát, on the party's 'undercover campaign on migration' and other party events where migration was the central topic.

On 28 October, Dániel Kárpát picks me up next to parliament. In a cheerful mode, he brags that he is one of the few Jobbik MPs that ever leaves parliament. 'This is my specialty. To meet with people face to face. That's what we are doing right.' In the back seat is his adviser, a 21-year-old woman named Natalia, a Jobbik youth leader from Misckolc. Kárpát has hired her to translate German press coverage of Hungary. As with many other Jobbik supporters I interview, Kárpát complains about 'Jobbikphobia' in the West and claims that Hungary in general is under attack by the Western liberal lying press. the text: 'The internationally coordinated campaign against Hungary.'

We are driving towards Martonvásár, where the forum on migration will be held. Kárpát, a keen drummer, plays The Prodigy, then Metallica on the car stereo, tapping the rhythm on the steering wheel while recalling his passion for the English electronic music group. Kárpát plays the drums and is a keen cage fighter, keenly emphasizing that he has interests beyond politics. He adds wistfully, 'I'm an accidental politician. I did not choose politics, politics came to me. There are the politicians in Jobbik that only sit in their office. I personally need to meet people. That's why I arrange events like this.'

'You know we want to restore Greater Hungary, that's why we're promoting the rights of Transcarpathian Hungarians', Dániel says while driving. 'The era of Greater Hungary was a long time ago', I suggest. Provoked by my comment, Dániel turns down the volume and replies: 'No, it's only a drop in history', emphasizing Jobbik's yearning for the past of the Hungarian empire. Admitting that his dream of Greater Hungary might not materialize, he says: 'I would love to live in a world where Hungary regains the territory we have lost. Reality is a different question.' For a moment, he looks thoughtful, almost troubled. Switching topic and as if reminding me of my privileged access to the campaign, he says, half-jokingly: 'So, how does it feel to be allowed into the inner circles of Jobbik'?

We stop in the outskirts of Budapest to pick up flyers from a flat. The title of the poster advertising the event reads: 'Illegal immigrants detained in Martonvásár – or the real face of migration?' The purpose of the meeting is to inform the local community about the alleged dangers posed by migrants. 'Fidesz is hiding the truth from the people, there are migrants in the local community and they are posing a threat. I mean, would you not be afraid for your daughters?' Kárpát asks suggestively, knowing that I have a family and two small daughters in Norway. A sense of unresolved tension hangs in the air.

We park outside a prison, where we meet the local leader of Jobbik Martonvásár. Dressed in a black leather jacket, he sports a shaved head, heavy moustache and golden jewellery. Kárpát, dressed in bureaucratic suit attire, later comments and almost apologizes for his rough looks, stating that Jobbik has a problem with recruiting educated and sophisticated leaders in the more peripheral regions. Inspecting the prison at a distance, we slowly follow the barbed-wire fence. A few construction workers, still working at around six o'clock, are standing at scaffolding while transforming the building into a prison for migrants deemed illegal. Kárpát walks along the barbed-wire fence in a military manner, seeming to inspect it. Through the fence, we watch seven young boys playing football. 'Look, they can't even play properly', Kárpát jokes, as if this banal judgement adds moral weight to their incarceration.

I follow Kárpát and the leader of Jobbik Martonvásár to a meeting with Fidesz Mayor Dr. Szabó Tibor. The mayor seems puzzled by my presence and I am not allowed to observe the interaction. I wait together with Natalia, Kárpát's assistant, in the local bakery in a downtrodden part of Martonvásár, a village of around 5,500 people. While we sit in the bakery with the few other customers, she reveals her anxiety about the large-scale migration. In German she says with conviction:

> They come here with their Koran, with their crime and the burka. See what happens in Europe. The terrorist come and spread their ideology and violence. I don't feel safe walking alone at night. We don't want Islam in Hungary. Islam is cancer. They are not refugees, they are illegal

migrants. I am sure that Hungary soon will be Muslim. People are ignorant who think they will survive this invasion.

I ask Natalia whether she has ever encountered a migrant herself, at which she shakes her head. 'Never, I would be too afraid!' For Natalia, and many other informants, Muslim migrants and Islam seemed to be entwined with cultural identities and historical trajectories far removed from their understanding of whiteness and Western Christian cultures. Both the 'conceptual Jew' (Bauman 1989:3) and what I term a 'conceptual Muslim' carry a message: that the alternative to the order here and now is not another order, but chaos and devastation. The fear of the Other in this perspective is based on the fear of impurity and disorder that allegedly boundary transgression will generate.

Half an hour later, Kárpát looks disappointed when we meet in the local pub, insisting that the mayor is hiding the truth from the people.

After a meal, we drive across a large, open field of brown-coloured grass as the sun is setting. 'This is no-man's land', Kárpát comments. 'No one can escape from here.' We visit a second, larger prison with around 1,000 inmates. Kárpát wants to inquire into the behaviour of detained migrants. At dusk we are greeted by two police officers and taken to a formal meeting room of heavy furniture and drawn curtains. It is dark outside and quiet inside the room. The police officers seem unenthusiastic about our presence and the meeting lasts for around 15 minutes. The fruit and soda placed on the mahogany table remains untouched, as if the Jobbik leaders are unwilling to fully trust the information provided by the hosts. Kárpát gives me a short summary as we hurriedly return to the car. 'They say that of 1,000 prisoners they have no trouble with the ten migrants. No problems? I doubt it.'

We arrive at the local cultural centre where a meeting is co-hosted by the local Jobbik branch. A quarter of an hour before the event only a handful of people have shown up. The local Jobbik leader is clearly nervous, anticipating a poorly attended event. Dániel invites me to a round of table football. He states that 'he [would] like to be a success', and seems more than discontent with the local organizers. His mood lifts up as the hall slowly fills with around 50 supporters. Dániel gives a speech similar in content to the one delivered in Haller Street. The migrants are framed as an existential threat to Hungarians and must be prevented from arriving in national territory.

The afternoon spent in Martonvásár struck me as an intense search for evidence about the alleged dangers posed by migrants. Kárpát blamed various actors for hiding the grim truth about migrants: that they were criminals who came to sexually abuse 'our women', conduct crime and spread radical Islam. The German media, the Norwegian researcher, the Swedish government, the Fidesz mayor, the local police officers were all untrustworthy sources of information regarding the 'real' dystopic nature of the migrants. Kárpát's securitization of migrants in the image of the criminal terrorist and sexual offender removed individual bios, reducing all migrants to 'illegal aliens', to disposable strangers. An objectifying gaze, observing the contained migrants at a distance and visiting actors to probe into their alleged criminal behaviour, were practices securitizing the migrants while establishing Jobbik as the protector of a nation in danger.

Following Fidesz's line, gendered, violent imaginaries of migrants from Muslim-majority countries emerged in Jobbik's politics of fear. By propagating similar grammars of exclusion, Fidesz and Jobbik reveal shared practices and politics. The emerging Islamophobia propagated by the far right in Hungary, coupled with Jobbik's ongoing effort to mainstream the party, have, at least on the surface, brought Fidesz and Jobbik closer in content and style. My impression is confirmed by the Jobbik MP and foreign affairs spokesperson Márton Gyöngyösi: 'Orbán or Vona, Vona or Orbán, it is difficult to know who is who these days.' I interview Gyöngyösi in parliament, located on the eastern bank of the Danube in the heart of Budapest. Gyöngyösi is tall and wearing glasses and a suit, his style markedly different from the more rough-looking ultra-nationalists I encountered in the countryside. Still, he is not less radical when he comes to ideas. **During our conversation he expresses his admiration for the 20th-century fascist Julius Evola,** a key intellectual figure for the radical right in contemporary Europe. The son of a diplomat, he grew up mostly in the Middle East and Asia in countries like Egypt, Iraq, Afghanistan and India. His office is decorated with Iranian and Turkish souvenirs. Fluent in English, he graduated with a degree in business and political science from Trinity College in Dublin in 2000. Gyöngyösi states that 'Orbán has stolen Jobbik's ideas'. 'The double citizenship laws was our idea. Influenced by Jobbik, Orbán has moved in a more patriotic and nationalist direction', he sayst. 'There is a battle over votes now. And Orbán wants to steal votes from Jobbik.' Gyöngyösi's worries, combined with wounded pride, were not unfounded. Jobbik had obtained one in five votes in 2015, leading Fidesz to portray itself as a defender of national interest, which also included a similar mobilization around xenophobic tropes and rhetoric.

Nurturing nationalist passions

'The freedom fighters drew their strength from the patriotic interwar regime of Miklós Horthy.' Gábor Vona, leader of Jobbik, the former history student turned Jobbik president, is standing at the podium delivering a passionate speech on 23 October, the national day of commemorating the anti-Soviet revolution of 1956. A crowd of around 500 Jobbik supporters is gathered in District VIII's Corvin Alley, a stronghold of the revolutionaries. Jobbik banners and red and white Arpad-stripe flags are waving in the light breeze. People of all ages are attending the event, from families with children to grandparents and youth.

Standing next to me are a few male members of the banned, but still functioning, paramilitary organization Magyar Gárda, first established in 2007 by Gábor Vona, that gathers and rallies for the protection of 'defenceless ethnic Hungarians'. In the crowd are also members of the irredentist youth group Sixty-four Counties Youth

Movement (HVIM), aimed at the establishing of Greater Hungary. They all listen attentively to the praise of Hungary's interwar admiral, Miklós Horthy, who ruled Hungary from 1920 to 1944. Horthy signed numerous anti-Jewish laws in 1938, 1939 and 1920, and was one of Hitler's closest allies. In Jobbik's view, Horthy was 'the greatest statesman of the twentieth century', a 'regent' that put Hungary on the path of prosperity following the disintegration of the Austro-Hungarian Empire after World War I. Since Jobbik gained power the party has erected numerous statues in his memory. The most controversial is placed in the heart of Budapest at Szabadság Tér (Freedom Place) outside the entrance of the church of the Calvinist minister Lóránt Hegedüs Jr, a notable antisemite and admirer of the British historian and Holocaust denier David Irving (Schiff 2013). Jobbik appropriates Horthy's memory to boost popular support and morale when faced with a new perceived crisis: the mass influx of migrants.

Nationalist music and emotional speeches nurturing nostalgia for a Hungarian golden age are delivered from stage. One of Hungary's most famous movie stars, Bernadett Gregor, performs, having publicly embraced Jobbik's nationalist solution as the best political path for 'her children's future'. István Bozó, the leader of Jobbik's London 'friendship circle' founded in July 2015, spoke about the serious problem of emigration and that many of the 350,000 Hungarians that according to his estimates live in London might not return home. Kárpát and Vona slowly carry a wreath between them, accompanied by emotional music, placing it at the statue commemorating the victims of the uprising.

After the ceremony, I interview Kárpát inside the cinema building. He seems proud and content, having just addressed the party's followers. I ask him whether there are any parallels between the situation in 1956 and today, as they are both periods marked by large-scale forced displacement. 'No', he answers categorically. 'You can't compare it. The migrants today have a radically different culture. We need to defend Hungarians against the illegal migrants.' The necessity of defending the country and European Christian civilization was a recurring motif amongst Jobbik leaders and supporters. Another concern was the fact of Hungarian out-migration and Jobbik leaders worried about ethnic Hungarians leaving the country. A sense of crisis and a nation under threat functioned to bring together a great variety of supporters – from conservative families to neo-facists – in their common cause to defend the Hungarian nation and Christian civilization against the threat of Muslim others. The Jobbik rally exploited the memory of past symbolic events to boost support for and morally legitimize present-day securitization of migration. The leaders reinforced the notion that the nation is threatened by a wave of illegal, Muslims others. Cultural difference perceived to pollute undiluted Hungary and its future generations rendered the migrants as 'human waste', stripped of their right to seek political and legal protection.

Figure 3.2 Jobbik rally in Budapest
(photo courtesy of the author)

White, ethnic Hungarian families to the rescue

While exclusion often was framed in terms of protection of Hungarian culture or Christian civilization, ideas about biological differences and phonotypes were also utilized in race-making processes. Discussing the migration crisis with a young couple in Martonvásár, the young woman Beata stated that:

> Europe has taken in billions of brown and black skinned immigrants. That is not diversity. We need to protect the white race, the people with white skin. Only they should be allowed to immigrant. If the dark migrants come they would get ten kids each. Do the math. We need to stop the illegal migrants.

Others invoked the notion of a demographic winter, emphasizing how whites were becoming a global minority and how Muslim migration would increase the non-white population. Europe was failing to compete in demographic terms with its main rival – the Islamic civilization. Prime Minister Viktor Orbán reinforced the view of migrants as a threat to (white) reproduction and security by conducting a 'national consultancy on migration and terrorism', that implicitly invoked shared whiteness as a basis of racialized inclusion. The consultancy asked all citizens above the age of 18 whether the Hungarian state should 'focus more on Hungarians and the children they can have' rather than migrants. In this gendered discourse, the prime minister defines a specific role for white women and families as the bearers and guardians of culture and civility. The future reproduction and purity of the white/Christian nation is put up against the flood of brown-skinned migrants from Muslim-majority countries. White skin colour becomes the criterion of inclusion in the community of Hungarians and 'real' European nationals, and thus requires the construction and reproduction of boundaries around the white, Hungarian nation.

At a speech held on 25 May 2017 at the opening of the 2nd World Congress of Families, Orbán continues his praise of traditional gender roles and the nuclear family as the central unit for the reproduction of the nation. He claimed that a liberal ideology is an insult against families and challenges Merkel's vision for an inclusive and integrated Europe. Linking issues such as illegal migration and terrorism discursively to Europe's declining native population, he said: 'For the future of Europe stopping illegal migration is imperative. This struggle – which is rationally justified – is only worthwhile if we are able to combine it with a family policy which restores natural reproduction on the continent.' According to Orbán, the very existence of Europe and Western, Christian civilization is threatened by demographic decline, fewer marriages and children and an ageing population. The founders of the conference World Congress of Families in turn claim that these unfavourable demographic trends are a direct result of feminism and homosexuality. Orbán's solution was to implement policies that would lay the foundation for a 'European population turnaround'. He declared the year of 2018 as the 'year of families' and proposed specific policies that would strengthen Hungarian families and stimulate birth rates.

In line with previous speeches, Orbán positioned himself as the strong defender not only of Hungary, but of Western, Christian civilization as a whole. He contrasted the nation's alleged inability to maintain a white, ethnic-majority population over time not only to lower birth rates, but also the arrival of refugees and in particular migrants from Muslim-majority countries. The public identity Orbán nurtures for Hungary is an anti-liberal, Christian conservative and white ultra-nationalist. In a populist fashion, Orbán contrasts the value-conservative illiberal democracy with the liberal, progressive consensus embraced by elites in Brussels and Washington. Orbán supported the Trump candidacy and he cheered for the victory. He claimed that Trump's inauguration represented the 'end of multilateralism' and a new era of 'bilateralism'. 'We have received permission from, if you like, the highest position in the world so we can now also put ourselves in the first place. This is a big thing, a great freedom, a great gift', Orbán said in enthusiastic support for Trump (Dooley 2017). In 2017, Viktor Orbán's former adviser Sebastian Gorka became President Trump's top adviser on counter-terrorism. A decade earlier, in 2007, Gorka tried unsuccessfully to found a new political party together with former Jobbik Vice Chairman

Tamás Molnár. Gorka was fired later in 2017 following the man who recruited him, Stephen Bannon. However, Gorka's tenure in the White House shows how a Hungarian radical nationalist remarkably moved from the fringes of Hungarian politics to the forefront of American far-right politics.

Orbán wins with radical right playbook

Fidesz's adaptation of ethno-nationalist positions traditionally associated with Jobbik has proven to be a recipe for electoral success. Viktor Orbán won a landslide victory in Hungary's general election on Sunday 8 April 2018, resulting in a third consecutive term for Fidesz. In speeches leading up to the election, Orbán stated 'we don't want to be colourful' and we 'don't want to be an immigrant country'. In his final election rally, Orbán stated: 'Migration is like rust that slowly but surely would consume Hungary.' The Hungarian government has even reused an image used in an anti-immigration Brexit campaign by Ukip, turning fears into votes. The image depicts a queue of Syrian refugees crossing from Croatia to Slovenia with a stop sign printed onto the image. Effectively embracing ethnic nationalism while rejecting diversity, Orbán challenged the core norms and values of liberal democracy.

While Fidesz has transformed into a fully fledged PRR party, Jobbik has used the past few years to change its grammars of exclusion in order to broaden its appeal. The party leader of 15 years, Gábor Vona, has long expressed his admiration for Islam and the Muslim and Arab world. Following the refugee crisis of 2015, Jobbik made a U-turn on its traditional positive stance on Islam, marking Muslim migrants as threats to the nation. While the figure of the non-European (mostly Muslim) 'Other' unites the Hungarian radical right, Vona has strived to moderate the party traditionally known for its antiziganism and antisemitism. Vona has posed with his arms around Roma minorities in the Hungarian countryside, the very people he dehumanized in order to gain political power. He has sent Hanukkah greetings to Jewish leaders in an effort to expunge accusations of antisemitism, and patted puppies to show a softer side to the party. However, it would be premature to interpret these recent shifts as evidence that Jobbik and Fidesz have switched places in the Hungarian political landscape. While a polished Jobbik appear more moderate on the surface, the radical ethno-nationalist agenda remains the same.

What is clear, however, is that Orbán rather than Vona had the winning formula insofar as the Hungarian electorate were concerned, securing a two-thirds majority in parliament with its ally, the Christian Democrats, with 133 out of 199 seats. Jobbik came second, but was unable to obtain more than 26 seats in parliament, perhaps indicating that nationalist voters did not trust the party's transformation. Vona promptly announced his resignation as Jobbik's leader, and the party will yet again have to choose what profile it should cultivate if it is to recover. But what is sure is that by adopting Jobbik's ultra-nationalist style of politics, Orbán has transformed Fidesz from a Christian

70 *Disposable strangers*

conservative party to a fully fledged PRR party. The side effect of this has been to curb Jobbik's growth. Fidesz's adoption of Jobbik's playbook shows that scaremongering over migrants and minorities works. Moreover, it highlights the effects of Orbán's dangerous dance with the far right, which has seen him embrace their agenda, jettison liberal values, and move Hungary further along a sliding path towards autocracy, all of which will undoubtedly present the EU with a major challenge in the coming years.

Re-inscribing bios

Not all Hungarians are passive consumers of xenophobic campaigns propagated by populist nationalists, by any means. The border-crossing act can also be a zone of creative potential for change. While the radical right spearheaded by Fidesz and Jobbik are exploiting a sense of crisis to bolster support for exclusionary ethno-nationalism, a minority of Hungarians are resisting governmental practices of populist securitization, re-inscribing bios to categories of people deemed disruptive to the utopian quest for purity and social order. Like in other European countries where state responses to the forced migrants have been hostile or ambivalent, concerned citizens express their solidarity in discourse and social practice (Herzfeld 2016:200). In the summer of 2015, when migrants gathered in public spaces such as railway stations of major cities (Szeged, Debrecen, Budapest, Győr), parks and city squares, non-governmental organizations such as Migration Aid and the Helsinki Committee took an active role in providing assistance, condemning the hostile state and societal responses. A month before I travelled with Kárpát, he was met by protesters from the human rights organization Freedom, not Frontex when he held an appeal at the border between Hungary and Serbia in Roszke. Ordinary Hungarians initiated campaigns on social media, raising funds and organizing activities to alleviate the human consequences of government policies. Such civilian initiatives demonstrate ordinary acts of compassion that insist on meeting the stranger not as disposable waste, but as human.

Some activists I interviewed drew lines from past atrocities committed against Jewish and Roma minorities to contemporary governmental response to migration. A controversial statue commemorating the victims of World War II diminishing the Hungarian state's responsibility for the systematic deportation and genocide of nearly 440,000 Hungarian Jews has led to fierce opposition. At Szabadság Tér, an alternative Holocaust memorial consisting of personal items, family photos, books and documents, built by children and grandchildren of Holocaust survivors, provides a powerful act of resistance against the government monument as well as the absence of the victims in the memorial. Since the erection of the statue in July 2014 there have been daily gatherings of intellectuals, pensioners, members of the Jewish communities and other concerned citizens, protesting the falsification of history (Kovács 2015). The protest I observe on Monday 12 October was the 553rd in a row,

Figure 3.3 The alternative Holocaust memorial at Szabadság Square consisting of personal items, family photos, books and documents, built by children and grandchildren of Holocaust survivors
(photo courtesy of the author)

illustrating the endurance and intensity of the resistance against the government's narration of history.

Orbán's populist anti-immigration campaign has prompted similar civic engagement by groups who want to bust myths about migrants. Grassroots activists raised 33.3 million forints ($115,000, €105,000) from over 7,000 people to launch a protest against Orbán's campaign. Hundreds of billboards mocking the state propaganda were set up with messages like 'the campaign of hatred loves you'. Other posters carried statements in English such as 'Welcome to Hungary' and 'I have survived the Hungarian anti-immigration campaign'. A sentiment shared by many Hungarians worried about the government's illiberal turn is summarized by the poster that says 'Sorry about our Prime Minister'. These examples of civic engagement show how activists and concerned citizens strive to unsettle state discourses about nationalism and immigration. Where the state showed hostility and made the migrants disposable, concerned Hungarians welcomed the strangers through discourses and practices of compassion. Moreover, these acts of solidarity reflect an ongoing struggle over values and identity in post-socialist Hungary, between a vision of inclusionary, open society that recognizes the Other and that of exclusionary ethno-nationalism that renders the Other disposable.

Conclusion

The enveloping crisis of displacement in Europe has impacted both European governments and societies, challenging its discourses towards immigration in general and Muslim migration in particular. The diversity of policy responses and intensity of emotion surrounding the humanitarian emergency have made clear the deepening polarization of politics and its challenge for social cohesion. This chapter has analysed the dynamics of far-right securitization of forced migration in Hungary and its contestation.

The illiberal democracy practised in Hungary under Orbán conceives of and deploys hospitality according to a logic that announces the 'host' and knows its 'guest' in advance of any visitation. In 2015, the Orbán-led government fiercely rejected the EU quota proposal forcing EU member states to accept an obligatory number of forced migrants. Accelerated migration from Muslim-majority lands functioned as a critical event through which Fidesz and Jobbik reconfigured their grammars of exclusion, presenting their parties as the righteous protectors of a nation in danger.

Contrary to Zygmunt Bauman's static conceptualization of forced migrants as 'human waste' deprived of value, it was precisely their conceived threatening economic agency that facilitated a space for their securitization in the image of the 'crimmigrant Other'. The economic arguments of the state-orchestrated anti-immigration campaign strategically tapped into the hardships part of Hungarian society experience. However, it was the discourses associating migrants with cultural pollution and crime that were invoked to justify their securitization as 'illegal aliens', categorically excluded from national territory. Through techniques and nurturing of conspiratorial fantasies, migrants were securitized as an existential threat to the Hungarian nation.

Although Jobbik, in contrast to PRR parties in Western Europe, traditionally has highlighted its link to the Middle East and admiration of Islam, the Muslim migrants crossing the border of the nation-state were fiercely excluded from any imagined community. Fidesz's sharp move to the radical right coupled with Jobbik's emerging anti-Muslim discourse brought the two parties closer together. By criminalizing migration, Fidesz and Jobbik asserted a renewed sense of order while reinforcing the symbolic and actual boundaries of Hungarian nationhood. Moreover, the Muslim migrant served as a convenient stranger for both Fidesz and Jobbik, which moved radical nationalism from the margins to the mainstream by presenting themselves as the righteous protectors of an endangered nation.

While the Hungarian radical right rejected the Others merely as 'dirty' aliens, concerned Hungarians contested racialized securitization and suspicion, re-inscribing bios to migrants deemed 'human waste' by the nation-state. Moreover, the contradictory interpretations of migrants as waste or value, burden or benefit, parallel struggles over statehood and identity in globalized Hungary between a society open to the Other and one that closes its borders to difference, on a sliding path towards an illiberal state.

Notes

1 In Sweden, which never has received such a large number of asylum seekers in one year, 163,000, the suspected attacks on asylum centres increased to 50 in 2015, more than the previous four years combined.
2 In May 2016 more than 7 million Syrians were internally displaced and the number of Syrian refugees in neighbouring countries had passed 4 million.
3 Across European contexts, parties long hostile to immigration, such as Front National, UK Independence Party, the Austrian Freedom Party, the Sweden Democrats, the Danish People's Party, True Finns and the Progress Party in Norway, have all surged in the polls, using the refugee crisis as a springboard to intensify their anti-immigration rhetoric and policies.
4 In July 2010, days into office, Orbán passed a law declaring 4 June an official day of commemoration for the Treaty of Trianon, the 1920 peace agreement resulting in Hungary losing two-thirds of its former territory. In a similar move appropriating popular nostalgia for Greater Hungary, Orbán passed a law making it easier for Hungarian minorities in neighbouring countries to obtain citizenship. The symbol-loaded actions are symptomatic of how the radical right appropriates national history in particular self-serving ways, moving radical nationalism from the margins to the mainstream.
5 A poll released on 8 October 2015 by Median public opinion and market research on Hungarian attitudes to the refugee crisis, shows that 79 per cent of the 1,200 respondents would like to introduce even harder measures against the migrants. Moreover, his hard line is supported by political leaders throughout East Central Europe, from Czech President Miloš Zeman to Slovak Premier Robert Fico and Polish Prime Minister Jarosław Kaczyński.
6 www.jobbik.com/vona_g%C3%A1bor_about_islam

7 The Roma community in Hungary is the country's largest national minority, comprising 5–7 per cent of its 10 million inhabitants. Roma Gypsies, Europe's largest ethnic minority, have been categorized as 'socially dangerous'. Deployed as the internal Other of Europe, the Roma have been subjected to deportation and statelessness, forced assimilation as well as incarceration and massacre. In Nazi-dominated Europe, itinerant Gypsies were, like the Jews, persecuted and targeted for annihilation on racial grounds. An estimated 258,000 were murdered in the Romani Holocaust *Samudaripen* (Weiss-Wendt 2013).
8 The website was one of the sponsors of Jobbik's undercover campaign on migration, with its logo printed on the poster advertising the event in Martonvásár.

4 The Swedish dystopia

Violent imaginaries of the radical right

Dystopian populism

At the heart of the various populist nationalisms of the twenty-first century lies a dystopic view of European and global integration, fearing the erosion of national identity and sovereignty. The radical right invocation of dystopia does not just set out a negative vision of the present: it uses the portrait of a nightmarish near future in order to launch its political critique of the present. PRR politicians warn about the dystopic conditions that will unfold if their political opponents gain or remain in power. The perceived threat and actuality of globalized crisis can provide fertile ground for dystopic, conspiratorial anti-systemic narratives that bring simple explanations and cures. Their rendering of migrants from Muslim-majority countries as the agents of dystopic futures is strikingly similar in many countries. I will in the following show how dystopias of Sweden were used by politicians and supporters of the UK Independence Party (Ukip), the Sweden Democrats (SD), the Hungarian Jobbik and the Norwegian Progress Party in their anti-immigration discourses, practices and narrative strategies. Despite clear ideological differences between the parties and the fact that the parties operate in different geographical and political contexts, all use dystopian imaginaries of Sweden to reinforce the boundaries of the nation. The chapter demonstrates how PRR politicians translated individual acts of violence into violent imaginaries of migrants from Muslim-majority lands. What I term 'the Swedish dystopia' not only entails a message of alarm and warning. PRR parties use the trope of the Swedish dystopia in their call for action against the Muslim migrants and minorities they claim pose an ethno-religious threat to the national identity, security and even (Judeo-)Christian civilization as a whole.

The Swedish utopia/dystopia

For the theoretical framework of my analysis for this chapter, I draw on theories of utopia/dystopia by scholars such as Gordin et al. (2010) and Boer and Li (2015). Boer and Li notes how utopia can be understood as a 'decentered anticipation of a future' as it searches for something vastly new and better. The utopian impulse expresses desire for radical change and ideal future: 'large-scale social, political, ethical, and religious spaces that have yet to be realized' (Gordin et al. 2010). Central to the utopian drive is the pursuit and promise of closure, completion and perfection. Dystopia, meaning 'bad place' or 'hard place' was coined in the late nineteenth century by John Stuart Mill to signify a state of being that was the opposite of utopia (coined by Thomas More in the title of his 1516 book, *Utopia*). Dystopian and utopian modes are interrelated as they both imagine or enact alternative, possible futures.[1] Utopias and dystopias by definition seek to alter the existing social-political order at a fundamental system level. Following Gordin et al. (2010:3), I approach utopia/dystopia as 'historically grounded analytical categories', as markers for 'conditions of possibility through which we can seek to understand how historically situated social actors interpret their present with an eye to the future that have yet to be realized'. Utopian and dystopian modes can inform social imaginaries. Charles Taylor (2004) defines a social imaginary as the way that social actors imagine their surroundings in terms of 'images, stories, and legends'; it is a 'common understanding' that leads to a widely shared 'sense of legitimacy'. Schober (2016) defines the violent imaginary as 'the social practice through which people reconfigure individual acts of violence into a matter that pertains to the nation'. Through narratives, performances and images, the memory of violence is kept alive and can be instrumental in calls for defensive action.

In this chapter, I refer to the violent imaginaries of Sweden mobilized by PRR parties as the Swedish dystopia. The concept of the Swedish dystopia captures the process through which radical right actors interpret and connect particular acts of violence and spatial identity through decontextualized rhetoric and discourses. What Tambiah (1990:750) refers to as the dual process of focalization and transvaluation distorts, abstracts and aggregates local incidents of crime into larger collective issues of national or transnational interest. In the radical right translation and transvaluation of individual acts of violence, violent qualities are ascribed to entire nation-states and categories of people, in particular Muslims, who are marked as threats to national identity and Western civilization (Brubaker 2017).

It is through processes of transvaluation that Sweden has gained visibility in global imaginary as a dystopian place where chaos, decay and criminals allegedly reign in the present. While Sweden has been a constant point of reference for radical nationalists for decades, it seems that the uses of the Swedish dystopia have intensified in relation to accelerated migration from Muslim-majority countries to Europe. It is not clear how the increase in immigration and rise in crime are related, but the radical right has effectively managed to establish a firm connection between the two. While Sweden is still a much safer place that most of Europe and the US, the dystopian images of Sweden are used to nurture moral panic about Muslim migration. PRR discursive strategies relating to Sweden invoke terrorism and violence associated with Muslim migrants, failed multiculturalism and social degeneration.

A key feature of the Swedish dystopia is its dual character. The very dystopia in the present or the near future is defined through its opposite – the utopian myth and nostalgia for Sweden as an ethno-racial pure nation (Hinde 2016). The Swedish dystopia is intimately related to utopian notions and visions of Swedishness. At the turn of the century, Sweden played a key role in the construction of the white race and was a world-leading knowledge production centre for scientific racism. The Swedes were praised as being the 'whites of all whites', and as a consequence, the elite of humankind itself (Hübinette 2013). Like elsewhere in Europe, the ideal of cultural and racial homogeneity resulted in discrimination, forced assimilation and dispossession of minoritized Others, in particular the indigenous Sami population, Jews, Roma and travellers. While there have been multiple studies revealing the state atrocities committed against minorities in the name of creating national unity (Andersson 2009), the fantasy or nostalgia for an ethno-racial pure Sweden still holds a central place within radical nationalists' imaginaries. The Swedish dystopia also represent a discursive strategy used to attack and undermine liberalism since Sweden was and is held up as a liberal 'utopia' (successful model of integration, welfare state, high standard of living etc.).The epitome of a lost 'People's home' (Folkhemmet) threatened by migration occupied a central position in the political campaigning of SD.

My own personal experience during fieldwork was indicative of the nurturing of fantasies concerning national purity. As a stereotypical 'Scandinavian-looking' female researcher, I was racialized and gendered as a figure embodying the pure Nordic. Although I am a Norwegian citizen, several of my interlocutors regularly complimented me for being 'Swedish looking', tall, blonde-haired and blue-eyed. The Swedish dystopia mobilized by the radical right is anchored in nostalgia for a mythic racially homogenous past and present, which is why it is powerful when mobilized. Examining threat discourses grounded in the Swedish dystopia/utopia can reveal some of the ways PRR parties re-narrate (Bhabha 1990, Wodak et al. 1999), re-imagine (Anderson 1991) and re-invent the boundaries of the nation. In the following section, I analyse some of the radical right discourses and practices pertaining to Sweden, followed by an examination of how PRR politicians and supporters used the Swedish dystopia to nurture the logic of a nation in danger and call for political action.

Swedish conditions

In February 2017, President Donald Trump said: 'you look at what's happening last night in Sweden', during a rally in Melbourne, Florida. Trump incorrectly suggested that a terrorist attack had taken place in Sweden the preceding night. He later confirmed that the comment was based on a Fox News airing of an interview between host Tucker Carlson and a documentary filmmaker reporting on the alleged surge in crime that had followed the influx of Muslim immigrants to Sweden. Trump drew on a persistent set of myths about Sweden – that it is fundamentally threatened by Muslim migrants.

Mediated violent imaginaries of Sweden often start with local incidences of crime that in turn are decontextualized through reductive interpretive frames by (far-)right outlets. The London chief editor of Breitbart, a far-right website that regularly publishes Islamophobic conspiracy theories, released in 2017 a book titled *No Go Zones: How Sharia Law is Coming to a Neighborhood Near You* (Kassam 2017). The former chief adviser to Ukip's leader Nigel Farage, perpetuated the myth that there are urban enclaves in Sweden where Sharia (Islamic law) is imposed by Islamic leaders on residents and the police and authorities have lost control.

The book cover depicts the Statue of Liberty wearing a burka and one chapter in the book is titled 'from Malmö, with rape'. In a dystopian outlook propagating stereotypical views about Muslim leaders and their followers, Kassam believes that Sweden and Europe is rapidly approaching Islamification and worries that the US is on a similar trajectory.

It is important to note that there are challenges with organized crime in Sweden, in particular in the suburbs of large urban centres such as Stockholm, Gothenburg and Malmö. Lethal violence involving firearms has increased between criminal gangs. In January 2018 Prime Minister Stefan Löfven said that he had not ruled out deploying the military to end gang violence (Husøy 2018). While the challenge of violent crime in certain areas of Sweden is real, the notion of Swedish no-go zones has helped propagate the impression of a country overrun with violent migrants. Instead of examining structural factors such as poverty and socio-economic inequality, so-called 'second-generation' descendants of immigrants, are collectively assigned certain innate violent characteristics.

At the heart of the Swedish dystopia lies the idea that Sweden is undergoing rapid Islamification. In Hungary, many of the supporters of the radical right I interviewed feared that Europe was on its way of becoming part of an Islamic caliphate in that this would happen in the near future. Propagating the 'Euroabia' conspiracy theory of the Islamification of Europe, several of my interlocutors believed that the refugees of 2015, whom they always referred to as 'illegal migrants', were biological weapons to spread Islam to Europe. Some of my Hungarian interlocutors went further, claiming that there was an alliance between Jews and Muslims, in which Syrian migrants had become the biological weapons of Jewish will to global domination and the destruction of Christian Europe. Many believed there was already a war unfolding between a violent Islam and righteous (white) Christian identity and for some the process of Islamification was irreversible. A male Hungarian informant (23) I interviewed at a Jobbik gathering stated the following: 'Sweden is finished. I say good-bye, Sweden. The Islamic invasion is advanced. The Muslim savages will vote left. Sweden is turning into Africa. Actually, it has become Northern Somalia. Ignorant Somalia where people have an average IQ of 65.' Others invoked the notion of a 'great displacement', that immigration trends to Sweden would lead to a demographic extinction event. They feared that native nationals would become a minority in their own land and that this would happen in the not far distant future.

Swedistan has failed. The ethnic Swedes will soon become a minority. I give it maybe ten years. These new Swedes will have the right to vote and that will be the end of Sweden. In my opinion Sweden is no longer a country I recognize. It is a country of traitors and cowards and turning into a solid base for terror. There will be a Muslim majority in Sweden in 2028. Then Swedish patriots will leave the country much as many white South Africans left theirs.

The alleged Islamification of Sweden is imagined to be carried out by Muslim men reduced to the image of the 'crimmigrant' (Aas 2011) or the 'rapefugee'. If white, blond women are racialized as symbols of ethno-national purity, the non-white Muslims are conceived as destroyers of purity through time by planting alien seed. Several of my interlocutors regularly referred to the Swedish city of Malmö as 'the rape capital of Europe'. One male informant in England in his mid-fifties explained:

Our women and children are dying because Sharia allows the rape and murder of non-Muslims. In Malmö, rape, theft and murder are the new norms. Syrians and Somalians rapefugees have arrived, stupid and suicidal Sweden. With Somalians invading Sweden no wonder it is the rape capital of the world. The Swedish children suffer. Ladies, get used to being raped.

The narrative reveals fantasies about the threatening 'hypermasculinity' of male, dark-skinned foreign men that threatened white women. Violent imaginaries of Muslim 'rapefugees' in Sweden were not only invoked by supporters of the radical right, but by politicians who propagated similar discourses in their construction of Muslim otherness. Ukip MEP Nigel Farage claimed, for instance, that 'Malmö is now the rape capital of Europe' (Campell 2018). While Swedish authorities do not publish the ethnicity of the perpetrators of any crime, including sexual offences, in nativist discourse all Muslims are framed as potential criminals.

Playing upon styles of emotion already in circulation, Farage transvaluated local sexualized crime in one national context, ascribing it to all migrants from Muslim-majority lands. The projection of the violent 'crimmigrant', male other, makes implicitly Judeo-Christian masculinity more desirable. Similarly, white lawfulness and morals are reinforced in relation to the allegedly innate criminal nature of the male Other.

The uses of the Swedish dystopia

In September 2015, as mentioned earlier, I did ethnographic fieldwork at Ukip's annual conference in Doncaster. The party protesting European integration appeared strikingly transnational when it comes to forming alliances with other PRR parties. In particular, the bond between Ukip and the SD appears strong, perhaps reflecting their cooperation in the European Parliament through the group 'Europe of Freedom and Direct Democracy'. At the Ukip conference MP Peter Lundgren from SD gave a keynote talk, highlighting the similarities between the two parties and his great admiration for Ukip leader Nigel Farage. 'It feels like we have become a member of the Ukip family. We have the same values; we are representing the same people, ordinary, working-class people.'

Ukip and SD do indeed share many commonalities. Both parties appeal to the lower-educated working class who feel alienated from mainstream politics. Both parties mobilize nativist notions of Swedishness/Britishness against minorities and Muslim migrants, and both reject the EU and cosmopolitan elites. During the 2010 election campaign, the party's slogan was 'Give us Sweden back'. Ukip obtained its electoral breakthrough in the general election in 2015 and Ukip's referendum campaign declared 'We want our country back'. Both slogans connoted the message that the nation is under siege and threatened by Muslim migration.

While the two PRR parties have bonded in Brussels, they differ in important ways. The SD has much more extreme roots than Ukip, founded in 1988 as a white supremacist group whose members wore Nazi uniforms to meetings. SD has since struggled to distance itself from its skinhead past and mainstream the party (Teitelbaum 2017). The current leader, Jimmi Åkesson, changed the party's logo from a torch to a blue daisy to soften its image. SD first entered parliament in 2010 with almost 6 per cent of the vote and increased its support in the 2014 elections when it took 13 per cent of the vote as the third biggest party (Hübinette and Lundström 2014). Ukip started its campaigning in the 1990s and became a significant challenger to the parties that have dominated British politics the past century – the Conservative Party, Labour Party and the Liberal Democrats – when it won the 2014 European elections.

In 2016, the newly elected Ukip leader Paul Nuttall was invited to give a speech at the SD Conference in Sweden on the invitation of Peter Lundgren and his colleague, MP Kristina Winberg. After praising the electoral growth of the SD, Nuttall emphasized the many similarities between the two parties as representing the antitheses of the old, establishment parties. 'It is great to feel at home.' In a textbook definition of populism, Nuttall claimed that Ukip and SD represent the authentic voice of 'the people' against the elites and the old establishment parties. 'We speak the language of ordinary, working-class people. We straight talk. That is why people are flocking to us. People want normal folks in Parliament that act, sound and look like normal people.' Nuttall expressed anxiety over the impact of demographic change on culture, welfare and security through a politics of fear that reinforced the logic of crisis-ridden nation in danger. His narrative reveals the dual character of the Swedish utopia/dystopia, as a tolerant and liberal nation that is in danger due to *too much* tolerance and political correctness.

> We love Sweden in Britain. We have always looked upon Sweden as a tolerant, open, liberal country, a country that has a lot to be proud of. But we look at Sweden and we fear. We fear because of the demographic

change. We fear because we believe that your tolerance and you have probably more tolerance than the vast majority of countries in Europe. Your tolerance has led to an acceptance of intolerance. I look at a country which over the years has been riven by political correctness. A country where you are forced to say: 'all cultures are equal.' Well they are not. A culture that forces its girls into marriage is not equal to ours. We are the continent of the democracy, the enlightened. We must again be proud of our culture. That is the only way we can get democracy back. We must do away with the political ideology of political correctness.

In Nuttall's narrative, seemingly contradictory feelings are made evident. He praises Sweden as a country of tolerance that is admired in the UK. In that way he confirmed the exceptionalist, utopian image of Sweden in the global, political imaginary, as a tolerant, good, prosperous and progressive nation-state that is embodying the best of modernity. At the same time he claims that Sweden's exceptionalism has gone too far. Too much tolerance, progressive values and multiculturalism are responsible for the social decay and threats facing the nation. Nuttall deplores the fact that the idealized role-model society no longer exists. Something is rotten in the state of Sweden, and all the social-democratic loveliness is fundamentally threatened by European and global integration. The Swedish, politically correct, colour-blind ideology of multiculturalism has paved the way for liberal asylum and immigration policies that are responsible for the uncontrolled continuing arrival of non-indigenous people to the UK and Sweden. In particular, Muslim immigration poses a threat to national culture. While Nuttall praises the Swedish tolerance, he appears concerned about the capacity of Muslims to 'integrate'. The enlightened Swedish culture was contrasted with stereotypical assumptions about the status of women in Islam, thus suggesting a civilizing tone. In contrast to other nativist politicians I met in Hungary who already stated that 'Sweden was finished', Nuttall remained optimistic and hopeful for the future. Instead of locating dystopia in the present, he invoked the violence discursively associated with Muslims in Molenbeek to warn about what could happen to Sweden if they remained on the too liberal and tolerant path.

A couple of weeks ago I took a walk in Brussels. In a place called Molenbeek, the centre of European jihadism. Molenbeek is a snapshot of everything that has gone wrong. It has been under the boots of aggressive, forced multiculturalism. It has created division. A ghetto where people come from foreign nations, they do not integrate, they do not learn the language. But the failed policy of multiculturalism is in coma. We should all speak the same language. When in Rome you act like the Romans. We have a fantastic future ahead of us. Ukip and Sweden Democrats are connecting.

Nuttall used the actuality of a minority of radicalized so-called 'second-generation' Muslims in the impoverished borough of Molenbeek to warn against the violence that might spill over to Sweden. Molenbeek has the highest concentration in Europe of jihadi foreign fighters. Globalized images of jihadi terrorism is conflated with the image of the Muslim migrant in European nation-states, imagined to be inherently fanatical and violent. Nuttall used the town as a worst-case scenario and discursively aligned with the failed ideology of multiculturalism and irresponsible immigration policy that threatened the nation. Nuttall further used the prospect of Turkey joining the EU as a scare tactic to support Brexit.

> Turkey is a country which borders Syria, Iraq and Iran, countries that harbour terrorism. Countries that would like to harm us. Ladies and gentlemen, our parties mean the same. Turkey has no place in the European Union. Immigration led to stagnation of wages, it is also putting British people out of work. You are in the same boat.

After nurturing worst-case scenarios of Muslim crime and terrorism that might spill over the borders to Sweden, Nuttall ended his speech by replicating the party's slogan: 'Believe in Britain.' Do you believe in Sweden? He asked the audience in an engaged and emotional tone. The audience replied with enthusiasm: 'Yes!' 'We in Britain also believe in Sweden and we will be right by your side until you prevail.'

The above demonstrates how crime committed by a minority in one context rapidly can be transvaluated and framed by PRR parties as part of a wider cultural, ethno-religious and even intercivilizational conflict. In Nuttall's narrative, the conceptual Muslim 'crimmigrant' embodied fantasies about violent threats to national purity and social order, the very fabric of society. Both Sweden and the UK were threatened by European and global immigration and the jihadi terrorism and violence associated with the free flow of bodies across borders. Like the Swedish dystopia, the Molenbeek dystopia, was characterized by its essentializing character. While there have been acts of jihadi terrorism in both Sweden and Belgium committed by a minority of radicalized Muslims, the violence and terrorism committed by a few are ascribed to all Muslims. The local set of circumstances and causes of processes of radicalization are left out in the political transvaluation of the event. The populist narration nurtures imaginaries of a whole place on the verge of a jihadi uprising, with particular towns being slums full of threatening and violent Muslims. Societal ills, such as crime, are associated with entire groups of people, in particular Muslims. The violence is framed as if it is an innate quality to Muslims, and ordinary British and Swedish citizens are framed as the potential next victims of violent 'crimmigrants'. The dystopian conditions that faced Sweden in the present and near future unless the SD came to power were framed as a temporary deviation from a timeless and good Swedish mode of democracy defined by social order and tolerance. In contrast, a bright future would face Sweden if its citizens followed the Brexit path and decided to leave the 'dictatorial EU project' with its freedom of labour and movement rules and 'take back control of the borders'.

Protecting a nation in danger

Conceiving a nation as endangered may evoke emotions of fear, suspicion or anger. The political use of the Swedish dystopia that contains such violent imaginaries seemed mainly invoked in an awareness and warning type of discourse that is aimed at forming a base for political action. The action will be to secure borders and securitize migrants that are understood by the PRR parties to protect the nation-state from further deterioration. When the PRR parties perpetuate a discourse of disorder and danger through the Swedish dystopia, they simultaneously appeal to nativism or exclusionary nationalism as the solution to decay.

Dystopian images of Sweden are used by PRR parties across Europe in their mobilization and recruitment strategies. Both Ukip and SD invoked the Swedish dystopia/utopia to portray migrants as strangers, criminals and undesirable others, as an existential threat to imagined sameness. Leaders from both parties embodied and voiced a utopian Swedishness and Britishness set against the alien 'crimmigrant' other. The Ukip Leave campaign for the referendum effectively nurtured imaginaries of hordes of foreigners that would overrun Sweden and Britain, among them rapists and ISIS terrorists. Protecting a nation in danger thus required Brexit – to leave the EU and its freedom of movement rules.

In the campaign leading up to the general election in Norway in 2017, Sylvi Listhaug, the immigration minister from the populist Progress Party, frequently warned that Norway must not allow 'Swedish conditions' to develop. The Progress Party is among the most successful anti-immigration, right-wing populist parties in Europe, being the third-largest party in Norway and is serving in a governing coalition in parliament. Established in 1973 as a libertarian, anti-bureaucracy and anti-establishment party promoting a reduction in taxes, anti-immigration has been a core issue of the party's platform since the 1980s (Jupskås, in Akkerman et al. 2016).

Running an election campaign that emphasized strict control of immigration, Listhaug frequently warned against taking in as many asylum seekers as Sweden. Like Breitbart editor Raheem Kassam, Listhaug perpetuated the myth that there are more than 60 police no-go zones in Sweden. Two weeks before the parliamentary elections in Norway in September 2017, Listhaug visited Rinkeby, a suburb of Stockholm with a high proportion of immigrant residents and affected by a surge in violent crime. Her stated goal was to learn about how local actors cope with the violence, but her visit can also be seen as an attempt at turning fears into votes. The Progress Party politician placed dystopia directly in a dark and depressing present, conjuring up an even darker future for those who did not support the party's call for stricter border control and anti-immigration measures. The message was clear: We don't want the 'Swedish conditions' to spill over the border. Campaigning heavily against immigration and using anti-Islam rhetoric and images, the Progress Party received 15.3 per cent of the vote, a bare percentage point lower than during the 2013 general election.

Similar strategies of fearmongering over 'Swedish conditions' were applied by Jobbik in Hungary. In contrast to the Progress Party politician who invoked failed multiculturalism, the Jobbik leadership first and foremost mobilized the Swedish dystopia in their categorical resistance to the influx of refugees from the Middle East. In 2015, I followed Jobbik's vice president and deputy leader of the party's Parliamentary Group, Dániel Z. Kárpát, on the party's 'undercover campaign on migration'. Kárpát, a keen historian, wanted to know whether I could provide details of crime statistics in Sweden, insisting on linking crime and terrorism unilaterally to Muslim migrants that were passing through Hungary on their way to Western Europe. Furthermore, he was keen to know whether I as a blonde woman received much unwanted attention from the new arrivals and if I as a mother was worried about my two daughters' safety. Kárpát's 23-year-old assistant was equally anxious about the threat of sexualized crime. In the narratives of the Jobbik politicians, the trope of the Muslim rapist was regularly used in their call to secure the border against 'illegal aliens'. Tropes like the 'rapefugee' can trigger deeply gendered feelings and identities, mobilizing fear in many women, and aggressor or protector responses in many men (Rachod Nilsson and Tetrault 2003:70). Where the 'rapefugee' is violently imagined to violate the racial purity of the nation, the nation is secured by race-pure women. The imagined rape by alien men of the female body/nation thus requires relentless vigilance to protect the endangered nation.

In 2016, Jobbik and their governing partner Fidesz perpetuated the myths about Sweden as part of a campaign leading up to a national referendum on refugee quotas. In an apocalyptic discourse conflating displacement with international terrorism and crime, scaremongering about Sweden's no-go zones were used to secure votes against the Franco-German quota proposal, forcing countries to take an obligatory number of forced migrants (Thorleifsson 2017). The campaign invoking the trope of the Swedish dystopia seemed effectual. My Jobbik interlocutors were keen supporters of securitization policies, using Victor Orbán's erection of a barbed-wire border fence along the Serbian border as an example to follow. 'Europe will depend on Hungary's strength. Sweden should start thinking about building a barbed border fence since their border with Sweden is 1,600 kilometres long and one of the worst-controlled borders. There is nothing racist about saying we want to control our own borders.'

Jobbik supporters I interviewed blamed present levels of violence in Europe in general and Sweden in particular on Islamic aggression, insisting that a border fence was the only solution to keep the nations of Europe safe. Other, more extremist far-right actors justified the use of violence in order to protect a nation allegedly in danger. The following ethnographic vignette fleshed out this insight, showing how far-right extremist supporters of Jobbik praised the violence committed by white, Scandinavian terrorists.

White masculinity to the rescue

It is 23 October 2015 and I am attending a political commemoration event with Jobbik. Vice President of the party Dániel Kárpát points me in the direction of a torchlight procession arranged nearby. He is going to attend a martial arts class, and apologetically warns me that 'some elements of Jobbik can be radical'. I walk down a narrow, poorly lit street lined with buildings on both sides. I notice the procession and join the hundred or so supporters walking in the night. A few minutes later I find myself surrounded by the fumes of torches at a concert with the nationalist rock singer Kalapács József.

Two young men are dressed in black bomber jackets, leather boots and military-style trousers. As members of the neo-Nazi Blood and Honour group, they have the slogans embroidered on their jacket sleeves. I enter into a conversation with two young men. They are somewhat puzzled by my presence as a foreigner, but classify me as empathetic to Jobbik's cause. One of the young men asks what I think of the event in Sweden the preceding day, referring to the 21-year-old Swede who had killed two schoolchildren and a teacher and seriously injured several others with a sword before being shot by police in Trollhättan. Sweden gets what it deserves, was the view of the young men, openly expressing support for the atrocities.

Figure 4.1 Neo-Nazis at a Jobbik rally
(photo courtesy of the author)

> The liberal leadership of Sweden claim to be human but it is actually the opposite. They are bringing suffering upon its people. This young man gave his life. There is a race war. The future wars will be bloodier. The victims of terror in Paris have been unable to defend themselves against the criminal migrants.

In their narrative, Sweden and Europe are already in the midst of a cultural and race war, with liberal authorities unwilling to protect racially pure citizens from dangerous non-white others. Liberal asylum and immigration policies have led to the rapid mass arrival of Muslim migrants that threaten national identity, security and the European white race. Later that night I go through the comment section on the extremist web portal kuruck.info with the help of a Hungarian-speaking friend, and it is rife with sympathies for the terrorist.

> I feel so sorry for the white guy. He was in his early twenty's and should have lived longer. He should have brought a machine gun. It is the liberals that are the guilty, they admitted the exotic people to Sweden and Europe! With Sweden filing up with Syrians and Somalis it is on the way of becoming a security danger for all of us. The liberal heads of the EU just stand still and watch it happen. When we identify Islam as a violent religion, we are called 'racist, xenophobes or Islamophobic'. When courageous politicians like Viktor Orbán tells the truth the liberals call it a hate crime. But there is nothing racist *about telling the truth.* Yes, Sweden is being destructed by the liberal establishment.

Another comment compares him to the Norwegian terrorist Anders Behring Brevik who on 22 July 2011 committed mass murder on Norwegian youth and labour politicians for being soft on Islam.

> They are both white patriots. The liberal establishment support the elimination of the white man through their filthy, liberal, multicultural, tolerant system. Sweden brought it upon themselves. Swedes voted for the liberals and deserves everything that is coming to them. The ethnic Swedes are so naïve. The end of Sweden started the very minute they opened their border. They just open the doors and thought everything would be OK. Secular liberals think that it is a virtue not to identify Islam as a violent religion. They are turning Sweden and Europe in to an Islamic hellhole! They ruined the life of this white guy (in Sweden) like a lot of white people have had their lives ruined. Clueless liberals should never be allowed to make decisions that advances the killing of innocent people. When society is brainwashed by the liberal elite, these brave men come. Without liberalism this young man would still be alive. Dirty liberals. But fear not, we will pay back with interest. Down with multiculturalism!

The narrative demonstrates a central trope in far-right discourse: that the Swedish liberal establishment are traitors responsible for the rapid decay of the nation. The liberal elites have sacrificed the purity and innocence of Sweden on the altar of multiculturalism and an ideology of antiracism. In response, brave citizens willing to sacrifice their lives must protect the ever-endangered nation. In the explicit endorsement of terrorism committed by white, Scandinavian men, violence is praised as an act of heroic defence.

By using discourse about white heroic sacrifice, the neo-Nazi supporters of Jobbik created both a Hungarian and transnational, unifying whiteness. The narrative strategies and practices of the two Jobbik supporters rely upon and reinforce the fantasy that Hungary has always been and must remain a white nation. Whereas only a tiny minority of my interlocutors endorsed right-wing terrorism, the message was clear: that the endangered nations of Europe are in need of protection in order to avoid a Swedish dystopia in their nation-states. Protecting a nation in danger comes either from a strong authoritarian leader or from vigilante activists that would protect 'our' women and children from the Muslims' 'invasion'. Moreover, the racialization of and violence directed at non-white, Muslim others served to make the pure Hungarian people white, by idealizing them as the defenders of a white culture under threat.

Conclusion

The findings presented in this chapter demonstrate how dystopian and utopian temporalities were invoked by PRR parties in their political campaigning. Across Europe and beyond, violent imaginaries of Sweden have become an integral part of radical right grammars of exclusion serving to re-draw the boundaries of nationhood. PRR parties and (far-)right actors use the Swedish dystopia as a central trope in their mobilization and anti-immigration strategies. Through the transvaluation of local crime, Sweden is violently imagined as a place of no-go zones ruled by Sharia law and criminal migrants. The Swedish nation is allegedly betrayed by the cosmopolitan, liberal establishment that strives to deny or erase national difference. PRR actors deploy violent imaginaries of Sweden in their resistance to immigration, Islam and multiculturalism, all of which they believe threaten the imagined purity of a national people. In particular, the refugee crisis of 2015 was used as an opportunity to spread conspiracy-based news, recruit new members and take actions against migrants from Muslim-majority countries they claim pose an existential threat to European, Christian civilization.

The Swedish dystopia plays upon older, racialized discursive traditions and is thus successful in activating certain affective structures. While the utopian and dystopian mode can inform social imaginaries, they can also be enacted in moments of sociality and actual practice. In Hungary, the Swedish dystopia was mobilized in the call for securitization of migrants and vigilante patrols along the borders. Some PRR actors justified violence and securitization by invoking violent imaginaries of the Muslim migrants threatening the race-pure Swedish and European women/nation. In particular, the nation-as-woman raped by Muslims and migrants was a violent imaginary invoked in calls for defending the body/nation's boundaries against invasion and violation.

The Swedish dystopia is defined in relation to its opposite – the utopia of the ethno-religious pure, good and innocent nation. The Swedish dystopia implicitly entails a protection, mourning and longing for the Swedish racialized utopia of a homogenous nation. A key feature of the radical right dystopian outlook is the warning that a particular nation-state will end up in the dystopia in which Sweden currently is cast. The Swedish dystopia thus emerges frequently in tandem with messages that conveyed the need to protect the nation against threatening others. The Swedish dystopia served at the same time to reinforce ethno-racial boundaries while propagating a nationalist solution: that the radical right is the righteous protector of a nation and civilization in danger.

Note

1 However, as Gordin et al. note, dystopia is not simply the opposite of utopia. 'A true opposite of utopia would be a society that is either completely unplanned or is planned to be deliberately terrifying and awful. Dystopia is neither of these two. Dystopia is a utopia that has gone wrong or functioning only for a particular segment of society' (Gordin et al. 2010:1). Dystopia as the utopia gone wrong has been reflected in literary works such as George Orwell's *Nineteen Eighty-Four* and Aldous Huxley's *Brave New World*.

5 Human waste in the land of abundance
Prejudice and ambivalence towards itinerant Roma

As a result of EU freedom of labour and movement rules, notably the Schengen Agreement (of which Norway is part, although it is not a full member of the EU), Norway has – like other European countries – become a site of new encounters between people who were formerly separated. Since the inclusion of Romania and Bulgaria into the EU in 2007 there has been increased mobility into the EU and related economic zones. The Roma minorities from these countries represent the poorest segments of European populations. Roma cross-border mobility is an adaptive response to poverty accelerated by economic recession. According to unofficial estimates, the number of itinerant Roma in Oslo on a three-month tourist visa is between 500 and 1,000, a rather small number when compared to other European cities.[1] Still, their survival strategies make itinerant Roma highly visible in public space. Many have appropriated parks, woods and abandoned buildings to create temporary homes. Facing enormous difficulty in gaining access to standard forms of employment, itinerant Roma subsist by various kinds of street activities, such as begging or informal work.[2] In Oslo, the relation between itinerant Roma and Norwegians is first and foremost defined through the very visible contrast between material abundance and economic deprivation. Poverty is low in Oslo compared to other European countries, and the itinerant Roma are significantly poor according to Norwegian standards.

In recent years, conflict has repeatedly erupted between itinerant Roma and settled Norwegians over the use of space, livelihoods and rights. Itinerant Roma are provisionally included and ascribed value by non-governmental organizations (NGOs) and concerned individuals. At the same time, they are fiercely excluded from any imagined community. In mainstream Norwegian society, including the state, as I will show, itinerant Roma are widely perceived simply as 'matter out of place'. With no intention or realistic prospect of being assimilated into their land of temporary stay, they embody ambivalence.

This chapter examines the dynamics and character of contemporary antiziganism in Norway. While the populist nationalist tropes of exclusion targeting Roma minorities might be familiar from other European societies, I argue that Norway differs in the centrality accorded to nature in its national mythology and identity. As the findings of the case studies will show, itinerant Roma are conceived by the PRR as well as other more mainstream state actors and media as threats to the established social order, but even more so to the purity of the Norwegian nature, which symbolically mirrors the integrity of the Norwegian nation. In contrast to other European contexts, such as post-socialist Hungary, I find that prejudice towards itinerant Roma in Norway is more linked to ideas about social purity than grounded in perceptions of threat to the wealth and welfare of the majority population. Confirming a basic idea from the theory of nationalism (e.g. Gellner 1983), this chapter shows that the boundary making of the government, a coalition between the Conservative Party and the right-wing populist Progress Party, has progressively rendered indeterminate social positions difficult to maintain. My data show that even populations rendered disposable 'human waste' by populist or state actors can be ascribed value and agency by various non-governmental actors. In the following paragraph I present some of the methods through which itinerant Roma have been dehumanized and excluded to identify historical (dis)continuities in techniques and tropes of antiziganism.

Antiziganism in Europe

If precarity can be basically defined as a structural economical and sociocultural insecurity, precarity is integral to the Roma minorities both historically and in present-day Europe. Living at the margins of the state, Roma, Europe's largest ethnic minority, have been categorized as 'socially dangerous'. Deployed as the internal Other of Europe, the Roma have been subjected to deportation and statelessness, forced assimilation as well as incarceration and massacre. In Nazi-dominated Europe, itinerant Gypsies were, like the Jews, persecuted and targeted for annihilation on racial grounds. An estimated 258,000 were murdered in the Romani Holocaust *Samudaripen* (Weiss-Wendt 2013). More than half a century after the Nazi genocide on Roma, *antiziganism*, that is discrimination and dehumanization of Roma, is thriving in a Europe hit by economic downturns, migration pressures and a marked swing to the right politically, and the Roma lack much of the symbolic protection offered to Jews after the Holocaust. Both itinerant and settled Roma face discrimination in education, housing and access to government services. There has been a measurable increase in hate crimes against the Roma, and the use of xenophobic discourse on Roma is integral to populist politics in a number of countries. As scholars have noted, the Roma serve as a pan-European symbol of the excluded outsider (Okely 1983, Hancock 2007, Stewart 2012, Farkas 2014). An estimated 10 million Roma live in Europe and are called so because of their shared Romani language, with many varying dialects. The contemporary state externalization of itinerant Roma as undesirable 'human waste' or 'exception populations' (Agamben 2005) that must be controlled follows surprisingly similar patterns throughout Europe. As the previous chapters showed, in Hungary, the ultra-nationalist party Jobbik, with an explicit anti-Roma platform, is currently (2018) the second-largest party in parliament. Both during my fieldwork in Doncaster, which has the largest Gypsy and traveller population in the UK, and in Hungary, the existence of an alleged 'Roma problem' has, since the onset of the so-called 'refugee crisis', been exploited by the Hungarian right-wing government to justify the exclusion of migrants from Muslim-majority lands.

While antiziganism is a well-documented phenomenon (Stewart 2012), less academic attention has been accorded its character and dynamics in Norway (but see Engebrigtsen 2012). Attitudes and exclusion processes toward itinerant Roma in Oslo are highly relevant not only for understanding social exclusion in the welfare state, but also to reveal some of the dominant categories of Norwegian self-identity, the culture/nature divide and cultural notions of the abject. My findings from the Norwegian context indicate that prejudice toward itinerant Roma is more linked to ideas about protecting socio-cultural purity, than perceived economic competition and fear of being outcompeted in the labour market. I show that the widespread association of itinerant Roma with disorder and waste is a key feature of contemporary antiziganism. In populist discourse and practice, Roma have been marked as a threat to the ordered and disciplined Norwegian body, indirectly helping to re-invent the boundaries of Norwegian-ness. The focus of the chapter is primarily not on the itinerant Roma themselves, but on how Norwegians interact with and perceive them and the ways in which these inform action. I now move on to describing and analysing the boundary work engaged in by informants in relating to itinerant Roma, identifying modes of exclusion. I show that the presence of itinerant Roma has generated ambivalent and hostile responses, including attempts by the populist right Progress Party to criminalize their presence.

Populist securitization of itinerant Roma

While anti-racist values and principles of tolerance have been an integral part of public education in Norway for more than half a century, the reception of Roma, like in most countries, has been ambivalent and largely negative from the government, which at the time of fieldwork in 2015 was a coalition between the Conservative Party and the populist Progress Party. As non-citizens, itinerant Roma are not entitled to any financial support from the state.[3] To alleviate their hardship, religious NGOs have established relief services for Roma from housing, clothes and food distribution to advice on how to cope in Norwegian society. Compassionate individuals have opened their homes and provided employment (NRK broadcasting company, 2014). At the same time, public discourse and practice toward itinerant Roma have been characterized by ambiguity or outright hostility. Roma beggars have experienced people kicking their cups used for collecting money and been rejected when trying to deposit bottles at stores, and provisional Roma settlements have been removed by force without prior warning (Anti-Racist Centre 2012, Djuve et al. 2015). Discussions on social media amongst individuals who subscribe to PRR causes have been heated, with participants referring to itinerant Roma in genocidal rhetoric, comparing them to the invasive Iberian slug, cockroaches or rats, in other words a pest which should be removed.[4]

For years, the populist Progress Party in the ruling government coalition has advocated for the criminalization of begging, a law that would in practice remove the dominant source of income for itinerant Roma. The party's main argument has been that begging is run by organized crime groups or is used to hide other criminal activity. In 2012, Siv Jensen, the leader of the populist Progress Party called for the forced eviction of begging itinerant Roma. 'Enough is enough, find a bus and send them out', she said in an interview with the national broadcaster (NRK, 2012). In September 2015, shortly before the local elections, the Progress Party politician Aina Stenersen claimed in an op-ed titled 'No, I don't have a krone' (the Norwegian currency) that begging caused crime. In another op-ed, MPs Harald Tom Nesvik and Ulf Leirstein claimed that itinerant Roma are organized criminals and both 'resourceful and relatively wealthy, in terms of where they come from' (NRK, 2017).

The Progress Party politicians all perpetuate familiar stereotypes of the Roma as criminal. A research report published in 2016, rejects the populist portrayal of Roma as organized criminals. Based on interviews with 1,269 respondents, the report concludes, first, that the beggars organize themselves in small groups, often families, and that they are travelling on their own initiative. The money goes to the repayment of debt (Djuve et al. 2015).

While research counters old myths and stereotypes, supporters of the Progress Party whom I interviewed about their views regarding itinerant Roma were largely negative. My ten interviewees between the age of 20 and 65 were in general not reluctant to express their thoughts and feelings regarding itinerant Roma. Many of them viewed itinerant Roma as a threat to the public order and the security of citizens. Some judged the itinerant Roma bluntly as perpetrators of crime, describing them simply as thieves and cheats. A 23-year-old man from the suburbs of Oslo, whom I interviewed in a café at Oslo Central Station, said:

> I do not understand how one can pity Roma. They have chosen to come here. Personally I do not give a damn about beggars in general. They are just ordinary people who do not bother to work for money. Not all beggars are organized, but most of them are organized criminals or work for organized criminals. So if you give money to the Roma beggars, you are directly or indirectly sponsoring crime.

His friend, a 26-year-old man, shared his view.

This has nothing to do with social deprivation. It is silly to defend organized crime. There are many naïve fools here in this country who let Gypsies take advantage of them. So no wonder why the streets are full of rabble.

Although several of my informants expressed aversion to Roma, they claimed that the issue was not racism, but fear of filth and crime. All themes show continuity in century-old stereotypes about Roma as thieves, lazy, dirty and immoral.

Polarized views

In February 2015, I met Natalia, a 23-year-old Roma from Târgu Jiu in Romania, the country where most itinerant Roma in Norway are from. She is sitting on the sidewalk next to bags of recyclables, begging for change. Initially sceptical about my questions and continued presence, Natalia shared information about her life. Natalia used to work in agriculture, but like other Roma, she was excluded from the unskilled labour market when domestic unemployment rates rose following the onset of the European economic crisis in 2008. In Romania, their housing conditions are typically dire, without running water, electricity and proper sanitation. In broken English, she explains: 'Things are so bad in Romania. I want to work and make money and help my family.' In Oslo, she generates income by selling the street magazine *Folk er Folk* (People are People), a relative of the British *The Big Issue*.[5] She spends the cold winter nights in a church run by the Church City Mission. With her, she carries a photo of her three-year-old daughter she had left behind with relatives. She lifts the end of her skirt to reveal worn-out shoes. During the coming weeks she calls me several times, sometimes crying. The winter in Oslo is cold, and she is looking for a woollen blanket. Another day, she is still coping, we walk her daily route. In Byporten ('The City Gate'), an upscale shopping centre attached to Oslo Central Station, she purchases hot water from a friendly Swedish waitress, pouring noodles into a paper cup, stirring with sticks aimed at coffee ten times the price. We sit down at a bench for a while. In the midst of our conversation, a private security guard passes by. Natalia freezes for a moment while turning her back to him. He approaches us, looking suspiciously at Natalia while asking if I (the anthropologist) am all right. Upon my confirmation, he nods firmly then moves away. Natalia quickly takes a few more bites of her sandwich before she utters with a sigh, clearly upset. 'They don't like that I am here. The man says go, go. I don't know why. What have I done? I am not a thief.'[6]

Natalia's story demonstrates many of the features of liquid life in a globalized Europe characterized by the freedom of movement and labour. She has planned in conditions of uncertainty, estimating both the burden and benefits of leaving Romania. She has to adapt to a precarious and unfamiliar situation and is depending on the host society and networks for basic needs like shelter and food. Then there is the dark side of liquid life. Itinerant Roma, with no intention or realistic prospect of being assimilated into their land of temporary stay, embody ambivalence. Moreover, they signify ways of being that challenge dominant conceptions of Norwegian national identity; they are unsettled, transnational, uneducated and without legitimate sources of income.

The Norwegian ambivalence to itinerant Roma was inscribed in the spatial design of the Evangelical Contact Centre, a foundation under the Pentecostal charismatic movement. The contact centre was initially established in 2012 as a low-threshold service for drug addicts and homeless people in Oslo. While the centre holds no official registration records, the leader, Stian Ludvigsen, estimates that more than half of the users are itinerant Roma and travellers. Every Tuesday and Thursday, between 400 and 600 people are served a hot meal.

It is a cold February Tuesday, and the line outside the centre is long. Surrounding us and manager Ludvigsen, in the middle of a large room, are some veteran drug addicts. A middle-aged man is sleeping with his forehead touching the table. A young boy dressed in worn clothes gratefully receives the meal of the day. White rice with minced meat and a piece of chocolate. 'He is our hero', says Maria, a Roma woman, touching Ludvigsen's shoulder, proud to know him. Many eat in silence, quickly finishing the meal. Others are chatting over coffee, not in a hurry.

The room is around 60 square metres, divided in two by a wall. The inner space is reserved for Norwegian citizens, the majority of whom are drug users. The space closest to the entrance is reserved for poor non-Norwegians, most of whom are itinerant Roma. For the Norwegian users, their drug addiction is considered only a temporary ailment for which the cure is salvation and guidance into better ways. They have a place in the nation-state, thus their stigma as outsiders can be healed, removed or cured into social inclusion. They can be recycled. The front room seats bodies of ambivalence. The itinerant Roma and other non-Norwegian poor are being shown the same human compassion and warmth, receiving the hot meal of the day and a bag of food past its use-by date. However, their seating indicates their imposed status as human waste, unwanted bodies not eligible for human recycling schemes. Even practices grounded in solidarity and compassion mark Roma as human waste. Not fitting into the orders of designed togetherness, the itinerant Roma are excluded from any imagined national community.

Providing emergency relief to itinerant Roma comes with a price. When the Roma first started to approach the Evangelical Centre in 2012, the leader noticed strong opposition amongst the contact centre's financial sponsors, the vast majority of whom are members of the Pentecostal movement. 'They wanted to give coffee and sausages to Norwegians only.' Torn between his personal conviction and the unwelcoming attitudes of the congregation, Ludvigsen turned to guidance and support in religion. 'I met the poor people standing at our doorstep. Those who line up for hours because they can't afford a hot dog at Narvesen [nationwide newsagent chain]. Those who eat from rubbish bins. I was frustrated. I took the Bible in my hands. I closed my eyes and let the pages part. The Bible fell open at Matthew 2:35–40.' He cites the verse: 'For I was hungry and you gave me something to eat, I was thirsty and you gave me something to drink, I was a stranger and you invited me in, I needed clothes and you clothed me, I was sick and you looked after me, I was in prison and you came to visit me.' He adds: 'I knew what God wanted.'

Based on his epiphany, Ludvigsen decided to implement an open-door policy, welcoming everyone in need. His decision to include Roma in the centre's user group generated negative responses from the financial donors, the traditional user group and the local community. Tensions between Norwegian drug addicts and itinerant Roma were initially considerable. An unknown neighbour was showing their resistance by pouring super glue in the door lock on a nightly basis, resulting in the instalment of a surveillance camera. Another person residing in the neighbouring building had on several occasions targeted the Roma lining up for meals with a water hose.

Another non-governmental actor, the Church City Mission, had established a programme 'space for Roma' (rom for Rom) to bust myths and misinformation spread about itinerant Roma by the populist right, media and wider society. Many migrating Roma are used to hardship and discrimination from the country and place they are from. However, they are often unaware of the Norwegian laws and policies. The Church City Mission taught migrating Roma how to beg the Norwegian way. They strongly advised Roma using begging as their main livelihood strategy not to touch people, as this would certainly invoke antipathy.

Another organization, Møtestedet (Meeting Place), run by the Church City Mission, had also registered tensions between Norwegian users and itinerant Roma. Initially the café was established in 2001 as a direct response to the challenges surrounding 'Plata', a relatively small, open space near Oslo Central Station, previously known as a market place for drug dealing, heroin in particular. Møtestedet was envisioned to provide an alternative arena than the streets for drug users, a place where one could engage in mundane activities such as going to a café without being marked with suspicion. Interviewing the leader, Kari Gran emphasizes that even though the café guests have multiple challenges, ranging from prostitution, drug addiction, and psychological problems, this is a place where they meet the 'whole person' over a meal. From 2009 onwards, a gradual change occurred in the profile of the users. Migrating poor, the vast majority without any drug-related challenges, would drop by sporadically. The number steadily increased. In 2010, around 10 per cent of the guests were travelling poor, in 2013 it was 19 per cent, and in 2014 this user group had risen to 36 per cent. As with the Evangelical Centre, the entrance of a new type of guest, that of migrating, poor Roma, caused tensions and loud resistance from the original user group. The manager had implemented separate service hours to reduce tensions. Both Ludvigsen and Gran noted that harassment and discrimination of itinerant Roma users occurred on a regular basis and turned worse during heightened negative media coverage.

Excess and expulsion

The desire for modern urban order has resulted in an increased emphasis on a clean local environment. Norwegian waste management and recycling schemes are deemed successful when it comes to removing waste. The value and communal obligation of producing a clean city is taught in schools from an early age. Since 1976, Rusken, a governmental organization, has engaged up to 200,000 people every year in volunteering activities to create a 'cleaner and more beautiful Oslo'. Adult volunteers and schoolchildren are given plastic bags, dressed up in fluorescent yellow vests and sent out to remove litter from the local environment.

Rusken has for decades been seen as the established authority of public cleanliness. Rusken is also partly responsible for collecting the waste from the abandoned or forcefully removed temporary Roma settlements in Oslo. From a waste management perspective, Rusken has repeatedly presented Roma survival strategies as scandals of pollution. On 5 October 2011, one could read in the online city guide, dittOslo.no, under the headline 'Barbecue dogs, and poops in the bushes', that 'garbage, old clothing, musty food, excrement and rat bones are tossed around. The smell of this mixture lies as a whiff of the area. Ducks and dogs have also been on the menu'. Rusken chief Jan Hauger expressed concerns about public health: 'The Roma defecate outdoors, often without cleaning themselves. Then they beg for money with which they later pay in the store', implying that the Roma are likely to spread disease.

Covering the same story, the liberal-conservative newspaper *Aftenposten* published an article with the headline 'This seagull was meant to be eaten'. According to the article, Rusken volunteers entered a vacated house at Grünerløkka, owned by the municipality, but occupied by Roma. 'When they arrived there were eight, ten or twelve Roma there. On the wall hangs a skinned dog, ready for grilling. The head on the floor. Those who cleaned were totally shocked.' Hauger emphasized that this was the only case where they have seen domestic animals being killed. However, he said that during the summer, Roma had begun to catch and consume rats, seagulls and pigeons, barbecuing them near the river of Akerselva. Needless to say, all three species are considered unclean among Norwegians.

In the bureaucratic logic of cleanliness promoted by Rusken, shared by the vast majority of ethnic Norwegians, human faeces outdoors are seen as a matter out of place, producing a sense of scandal. 'Human waste' making waste visible disturbs the ideal of a clean city and the flow of municipal waste management. The Rusken action attributes disease and dirtiness to itinerant Roma accused of posing a threat to public health. Rather than discussing the structural conditions leading to the precarious situation of Roma, the newspaper produced an unequivocally negative portrayal of Roma as dirty waste producers and consumers of unclean animals. Whether the latter practice actually took place is doubtful, owing to the strict purity rules for food that most Roma adhere to and that would not allow them to consume animals such as rats and dogs, which are considered polluting. Although the statements and allegations of the Rusken chief Hauger were partly refuted, such postings may nevertheless contribute to fuel prejudice.

In particular, the presence of Roma who have set up makeshift camps around Lake Sognsvann just outside the city has been a heated topic in public discourse. Located on the outskirts of the city, the area is used extensively for recreational purposes. The disproportionate attention given to Sognsvann in comparison to urban spaces where Roma have set up camps might be due to the valorization of nature, forming a central aspect of dominant ideas of Norwegian-ness.

Due to its close proximity to Oslo and easy access by public transport, Sognsvann can credibly be regarded as a space transgressing established norms for the ideal social use of nature in Norwegian identity. For around two decades, it has been used as a meeting place for people, mainly gay men, who solicit anonymous sex.[7] The newspaper headline 'You can't go anywhere without stepping on condoms' reflects the alleged problem of litter caused by gay sexual activity. While this practice might create a similar sense of scandal of pollution to the Roma untidiness, it does not challenge Norwegian national identity. Human waste disturbing nature and making waste visible is considered far more socially unacceptable and threatening to national landscapes, norms and identity than mere littering. A white 35-year-old Norwegian man working in the financial sector from the western part of Oslo shared his sentiment during an interview.

> I like running in the woods, but for a long time now I have avoided Sognsvann. The Roma settlements there are really disgusting, with faeces all over the place. It would be nice if they actually bothered to buy toilet paper, at least if they could find a dustbin. It is absolutely terrible. I just wonder why one must spoil the surroundings just because one is poor and homeless ... Why can't one keep it a little neat, just to keep some sense of integrity? I think it is quite natural that Roma are looked down on when they behave in such a way that they are bothering the rest of society. Had they at least showed some willingness or ability to adapt, I don't think they would have faced as many troubles as they do today.

In his view, the Roma survival strategies, which include setting up makeshift camps in the forest, disrupt his weekly routine of recreation in the forest. He judges them as being undisciplined and dirty campers, tying neatness and cleanliness to moral values and integrity. Blaming the stigmatized for their behaviour, he effectively establishes himself as a 'clean' and righteous citizen versus the 'dirty' outsiders who 'are bothering society'.

Several of my interviewees mentioned the Roma's embodied way of being as sources of revulsion. A store manager in his mid-fifties said the following: 'They really smell, they don't clean, they don't shower. I don't know if they have washed their hands. I serve them, but sometimes I tell them to stay outside of the shop.' For the store manager the apparent repulsive fragrance of the Roma signified disruptive otherness.

Other interviewees mentioned scandals of litter and pollution as a source of disgust. A female interviewee (63), a store employee and Progress Party voter, said the following:

> I swear, once I went to Sognsvann it was like Calcutta. There were bottles, bags and faeces. They are using the forest as a toilet. I know they have to poo somewhere. But then, they don't shower, they look dirty and they smell. I'm guessing they don't have that many opportunities to shower. It's not like I'm not caring for other people. It's just that I don't want them to live next to my house. Now I can't walk with my dog in the morning. If I see gypsies, I turn.

Associating Roma with the threat or actuality of waste was a shared characteristic of Norwegian antiziganism. While expressing concerns with what they viewed as humiliating and disruptive livelihoods, their revulsion would quickly turn to exacerbated prejudice or discrimination. In general, camping in the forest or mountains is seen as a quintessential Norwegian activity strengthening the central value of nature's purity in the national identity. Leaving rubbish behind after a camping trip is frowned upon. The Roma thus pollute not only nature, but they also pervert the sacred Norwegian relationship to nature.

Itinerant Roma as disturbance

The ambivalence to the presence of itinerant Roma in highly valued nature has also prompted legal disputes. In June 2013, Statsbygg, the Norwegian government's key adviser in construction and property affairs, proposed the enforced removal of Roma camps around Sognsvann, stating that they caused pollution in 'Norwegian nature' and posed a threat to public health. The call for eviction followed a visit by Oslo municipality on 10 October 2012, when an infection-control doctor stated that drainage of surface water from the camps could contaminate the water in the south-western part of Lake Sognsvann and thus pose a public health threat. Initially, the district court (Oslo Byfogdembete) declined the claim, noting that the 'pollution aspect was fairly modest in light of the submitted photos' and could not be characterized as 'substantial damage or inconvenience'.[8]

Statsbygg appealed to the district court. In September 2013, the district court deemed the camps illegal according to the Outdoor Recreation Act, which states that 'camping or another form of residence is not permitted for more than two days at a time without the permission of the owner or user'.[9]

Around 40 Roma migrants where given 48 hours' notice to leave the camp deemed illegal. The camp was dismantled at 09:30 in the morning and the makeshift tents were carried away in garbage trucks.

The case shows how the argument first triggering political action towards itinerant Roma was based on speculation about potential health hazards and pollution in Norwegian nature. While the court deemed the actual waste produced by Roma not to be a sufficient cause for forced eviction, waste in presumably unspoiled nature was judged misplaced in the moral sense of inappropriateness producing a sense of scandal. Attributing disease and dirtiness to the Roma settlement became a central means to demarcate the boundaries of the ordered and clean Norwegian nature. The garbage trucks sent by the municipality efficiently removed human waste, fulfilling its modernist promise. The clean-up operations at Sognsvann can be analysed as purifying events aimed at reinstalling the order of Norwegian landscapes. By removing the daily reminders of disruptive otherness, settled Norwegians are allowed physical and moral escape from (human) waste, the dark and shameful secret of modernity. In the dominant Norwegian understanding, nature is clean, fresh and genuine, as opposed to the seductive falsehoods of culture. Their transgression of the culture/nature boundary, along with their unsettledness, negligible contribution to the Norwegian economy and lack of something 'meaningful to do', shows in no uncertain terms why Roma are dangerous, superfluous people who visit without asking or being asked, leaving a trail of rubbish and human excrement behind.

Conclusion

For centuries, Roma Gypsies, Europe's largest ethnic minority, have been categorized as 'socially dangerous'. Viewed generally, contemporary antiziganism can be seen as a feature of the re-nationalization processes militating against the parallel processes towards European and global integration, which are seen in the rise of PRR parties in Europe. Norway, re-insulated from economic downturns because of its oil and gas wealth, has been dominated by culturalist accounts of difference rather than discourses of economic uncertainty. Although Roma, as Romanian citizens, can freely travel to Norway under the Schengen Agreement, it is clear that some migrating bodies are more desirable than others. Migrants who are like the imagined 'us' – the white, cultured, skilled, productive and healthy – are deemed worthy of inclusion into a new social body. Those who are like 'them' – the ones deemed uncivilized, unskilled, the poor, dirty and unproductive – are undesirable migrants, deemed threatening to 'our way of life'.[10]

In the capital of Oslo, the presence of 'human waste' in the form of homeless, begging Roma, the embodied daily reminders of European precarity, has produced hostile discourses, the acts of compassion described in the chapter being the exception and not the rule. In particular the populist

Progress Party, a coalition partner in government, has an openly and unequivocally negative stance on the Roma presence.

As I have shown, discourses on cleanliness, order and security have veiled and legitimized antiziganism. In the discourse of populist Progress Party politicians and supporters, itinerant Roma were framed as profit-seeking, organized criminals that posed a threat to Norwegian security and well-being. In both populist and more mainstream discourses, Roma have been associated with physical dirt and disorder as well as with humiliating lifestyles and livelihoods. In particular, the actual and perceived association of itinerant Roma with scandals of waste and pollution has contributed to their dehumanization and discrimination. Roma transgress the boundary between culture and nature established in Norwegian nationalism and reject the values and practices of majority society. They are quintessentially 'matter out of place' that do not fit into the self-understanding of Norwegians as hard-working, nature-loving Protestants who jealously guard the boundaries between nature and culture.

Notes

1 The number of migrating Roma in Norway changes according to the season and other factors, such as access to the unskilled labour market in their home country or other European countries. The majority of Romanian citizens in Norway self-identify as Roma or Tiani Romanian. They often speak Romanian besides their mother tongue (Engebrigtsen 2012).
2 Begging on average generates a daily income between 100 to 200 Norwegian kroner (NOK, £5 to £20), sometimes more. This is a substantial amount of money when compared to the income level in Romania, where the daily salary of a teacher is around 50 NOK (£5). The surplus is sent as remittances to the family and relatives, aimed at covering expenses such as food, health care, schooling and housing.
3 The established Roma, who arrived in Norway from Romania in the late nineteenth century, are entitled to state support, being citizens.
4 www.facebook.com/groups/229190177223730/?fref=ts.
5 The NGO Folk er Folk (People are People) was established in March 2012 to advocate for Roma rights, fight prejudice and provide employment below the tax line of 4,000 NOK. In June 2012 the street magazine *Folk er Folk* was launched modelled after *=Oslo* (a magazine sold by Norwegian drug users), as a measure to provide an alternative to begging. The organization has been criticized by expert in labour law Sverre Langfeldt, for not taking on formal responsibility for labour by itinerant Roma commissioned by private individuals or companies.
6 Thorleifsson tried several times to get an interview with the private security firm Nokas, but no one wanted to go on the record.
7 According to the organization of the promotion of gay and lesbian health, around 1,000 condoms are distributed monthly around the Sognsvann area.
8 www.domstol.no/globalassets/upload/obyf/internett/aktuelt/kjennelser/18_kjennelsem idlertidigforfoyningikketatttilfolge_33224066.pdf.
9 www.regjeringen.no/en/dokumenter/outdoor-recreation-act/id172932/.
10 Islamophobia is also on the rise in Norway, but will not be dealt with in this context.

Conclusion

This book has explored the appeal and grammars of exclusion propagated by PRR parties and their supporters across Europe. Examining different sociocultural, economic and historical contexts in England, Hungary and Norway, I have explored the various factors that drive local support for populist nationalism as well as the tropes and themes propagated by the parties. Contrary to research that claims that 'it's not the economy', I have argued that economy and material conditions do matter. Moreover, I suggest that cultural identity cannot neatly be separated from economic conditions.

In Doncaster, out of the tough mining life emerged a particular kind of identity and pride around the very insecurities associated with industrial work and the community experience, not just in the mines, but elsewhere. With the closing of the coal mines, Doncastrians I met thus expressed a sense of painful loss, over identity, meaning and community. Their common working experiences in the past were key in shaping a sense of culture *and* in constituting a sense of dignity and recognition. My interlocutors, in particular from the older generation, compared their life today with the life they experienced before the decline started three decades ago. They expressed anxieties over being made redundant in a precarious labour market. They were anxious about the fast processes of change that they felt had affected their town and working lives largely negatively. They were anxious about the speed of demographic change; about the impact of European integration and migration on their welfare, jobs and way of life. In Doncaster, the figure marked as the threatening other was that of the Polish labour migrant, whom they claimed stole jobs and resources that rightfully belonged to British nationals. In short, my interlocutors did not clearly distinguish between cultural and economic grievances. However, they felt strongly that their grievances and uncertainties in everyday life were ignored by the political establishment. While local supporters of Ukip primarily expressed concern about the impact of European integration upon their jobs, welfare and culture, the party racialized these grievances through an elevated politics of fear that marked Muslim migrants as ethno-religious threats to imagined sameness.

Like in Doncaster, discourses of economic insecurity and uncertainty of work were also propagated by PRR parties and their supporters in Hungary.

It was the framing of migrants as economic threats to Hungarian jobs that facilitated their further racialization as disposable, 'crimmigrant' others. In state campaigns propagated by the increasingly Islamophobic and authoritarian Orbán, Muslim migrants were framed as existential threats to the white nation and Christian civilization. Old antisemitic tropes, talking of Soros's wealth and power, are fused together with Islamophobic warning that the Jew wants to Islamize Europe. Such conspiratorial thinking about a Jewish masterplan to take over Christian Europe with uncontrolled migration from Muslim lands illustrates how antisemitism and Islamophobia are reconfigured by globalization with the purpose of reinforcing the racialized boundaries of the nation. New layers of meaning are added to older grammars of exclusion, revealing intersecting processes of racialization targeting minoritized Others.

In Norway, characterized by prosperity and a robust welfare state, the anti-immigration and anti-minority discourses propagated by the neoliberal Progress Party focused on cultural accounts of difference rather than on economic grievance. Drawing on a deep, historical reservoir of anti-immigrant sentiment, my informants justified antiziganism through the ostensibly apolitical deployment of the language of nation, culture and nature.

While the Progress Party and Ukip have worked to moderate their message and rhetoric, other parties, such as Fidesz in Hungary, have further radicalized their politics and rhetoric against Muslims, migrants and diversity. Compared to parties like Fidesz and Jobbik in the Eastern European context, the Progress Party's anti-Islam and anti-Roma rhetoric is restrained. While the local material and cultural specificities for hatreds or intolerance might be very local, the discursive expression of exclusion is strikingly similar across national contexts. The rhetorical strategies of PRR parties, as expressed both online and offline, continue to use age-old rhetoric and violent imaginaries of ethno-religious difference. Like the Hungarian radical right, the Norwegian populist right party framed Muslims and Roma as violent, polluting and criminal threats to national identity and security.

While some factors in the rise and appeal of populist nationalism are country and context specific, some common themes emerge in their proposed solutions. Parties like Ukip, Fidesz, Jobbik and SD, as well as President Trump, promise to protect the nation from the threatening other, and restore a sense of purpose to people who feel battered by forces outside their control. The populist nationalist parties exploited the anxieties caused by the prolonged crises of economy displacement, security and governance. Playing upon the fears and longings of a disillusioned electorate, these actors promise to defend their supporters against threatening immigrants and reinstall a sense of security.

The parties claim to provide better futures modelled around an idealized past and the 'good old days'. The PRR parties pledge to reinforce territorial boundaries, to stand up for 'the little people' against the elites, and to protect them against threatening others who are often defined in religious or racial terms. At the same time they project on migrants and selected minorities the total sum of fear, discontent and insecurities associated with the fast changes that have occurred over the past three decades. Historically, Jews, Muslims and Roma have faced similar accusations, racist tropes and persecution. As I have shown throughout the book, these categories of belonging are still marked in populist radical right discourses as 'enemy strangers', partly as a projection surface to imagine the pure insiders, those who rightfully belong to the nation. This appeared as a powerful formula to my interlocutors, many of whom expressed a mixture of nostalgia for the past and anxiety in response to a fast-changing world.

The surge in support for PRR parties poses increasingly strong challenges to the political establishment across Europe and North America. PRR parties have demonstrated that they now can win key electoral battles. The grievances that have enabled the rise of populist nationalism – a sense of cultural dislocation, feelings of relative economic deprivation and accelerated migration – are likely to persist. The increased salience of demographic change, the growing public anxiety over the role and perceived integration of Muslim communities, and dissatisfaction with the mainstream parties and European institutions will continue to cultivate opportunities for populist nationalists. In Hungary, the governing PRR parties that openly embrace ethnic nationalism pose a challenge to liberal democracy and the conventions, freedoms and values that sustain it. Viktor Orbán has embraced illiberal democracy, pushing the country in an increasingly authoritarian direction. While Hungary continues to enjoy the benefits of the EU, its leadership rejects the liberal values upon which the union is founded. Orbán is praised in other countries in the region, in particular in Poland, where the leader of the PiS, Jaroslaw Kaczynski, has hailed the illiberal democracy as a model state.

Another effect of their rise is that other conventional parties draw their policy agenda and rhetoric further to the right. While support for Ukip plummeted after Brexit, its effect reconfigured British politics. The rise of Ukip was a central reason why the Conservative Government decided to hold the EU referendum and it influenced the Tory agenda. Now that Prime Minister Theresa May is committed to Brexit and has highlighted the importance of creating opportunities for those who feel left behind, it is far from clear whether Ukip's new leadership will be able to spark the same sense of purpose that gave the party its previous momentum.

In Norway, the Progress Party lost little electoral support when serving in the governing coalition and has influenced other parties, including the Labour Party, who have moved their political policy agenda and rhetoric to the right. However, a more worrying effect is that xenophobic political campaigns can inform attitude and action. A troubling pattern of xenophobia targeting migrants and minorities has increased both in Brexit Britain, Trump's US and in illiberal Hungary where radical nationalists feel emboldened by political events and victories.

Europe is experiencing increasing stress as it struggles to find unified solutions to the crises of economy and displacement. Mainstream politicians need to better address the concerns of the citizens who feel fearful, left behind or not recognized in an accelerating world. However, rather than adopting the divisive rhetoric and causes of the populist radical right, conventional parties should challenge their policy proposals. All the crises perceived as existential threats precipitate different forms of response: how to reduce inequality, how to live with diversity and intersecting displacements and needs addressing of underlying political-economic structures rather than quick fixes. While insecurities caused by fast change have led to the heating of identity politics, the current historical juncture can also offer ways of imagining other, better futures and ways of being in relation to others. If conventional parties fail to seize the opportunity to reconnect with disillusioned voters and generate compelling visions for the future, then surely the populist radical right will continue to do so.

References

Aas, Katja Franko (2011) 'Crimmigrant' bodies and bona fide travelers: Surveillance, citizenship and global governance. *Theoretical Criminology* 15(3): 331–346.
Agamben, Giorgio (2005) *State of Exception*. The University of Chicago Press.
Akkerman, T., de Lange, S.L. and Rooduijn, M., eds (2016) *Radical Right-Wing Populist Parties in Western Europe: Into the Mainstream?* London: Routledge.
Anderson, Benedict (1991) *Imagined Communities*. London: Verso.
Andersson, Jenny (2009) Nordic Nostalgia and Nordic Light: the Swedish model as Utopia 1930–2007. *Scandinavian Journal of History* 34(3): 229–245.
Antirasistisksenter (Anti-Racist Centre) (2012) *Tilreisende rom i Oslo* (Itinerant Roma in Oslo). Oslo: Antirasistisk senter.
Ashcroft, Michael (2012) They're Thinking What We're Thinking: Understanding the UKIP temptation. *Lord Ashcroft Polls*, 18 Dec. Web. 18 January 2018.
Barker, M. (1981) *The New Racism: Conservatism and the Ideology of the Tribes*. London: Junction.
Barth, Fredrik (1952) The social organization of a pariah group in Norway. *Norveg* 5: 125–144.
Barth, Fredrik (1969) *Ethnic Groups and Boundaries: The Social Organization of Cultural Difference*. Long Grove: Waveland Press.
Bauman, Zygmunt (1989) *Modernity and the Holocaust*. Cornell University Press.
Bauman, Zygmunt (1998) *Globalization: The Human Consequences*. New York: Columbia University Press.
Bauman, Zygmunt (2004) *Wasted Lives: Modernity and its Outcasts*. London: Polity Press.
Benbassa, E. (2007) Xenophobia, Anti-Semitism, and Racism. In M. Bunzl, ed., *Anti-Semitism and Islamophobia: Hatred Old and New in Europe*. Chicago: Prickly Paradigm Press.
Benbassa, Esther and Attias, Jean-Christoph (2004) *The Jew and the Other*. Cornell: Cornell University Press.
Beresford, Richard (2013) *Coal, Coal Mining and the Enterprise Culture: A Study of Doncaster*. PhD thesis, University of Warwick.
Berezin, M. (2009) *Illiberal Politics in Neoliberal Times. Culture, Security and Populism in the New Europe*. Cambridge: Cambridge University Press.
Bhabha, H.K., ed. (1990) *Nation and Narration*. London: Routledge.
Bíró-Nagy, A. and Róna, D. (2013) Rational Radicalism: Jobbik's Road to the Hungarian Parliament. In G. Mesežnikov, O. Gyárfášová and Z. Bútorová, eds, *Alternative*

Politics?: The Rise of New Political Parties in Central Europe. Bratislava: Institute for Public Affairs, 149–183.

Blee, Kathleen (2002) *Inside Organized Racism: Women in the Hate Movement*. Berkeley: University of California Press.

Blee, Kathleen (2007) Ethnographies of the Far Right. *Journal of Contemporary Ethnography* 36(2): 119–128.

Boda, Zs., Szabó, G., Bartha, A., Medve-Bálint, G. and Vidra, Zs. (2015) Politically Driven: Mapping Political and Media Discourses of Penal Populism – The Hungarian Case. *East European Politics and Societies*, Online. First published on 4 December 2014 as doi:10.1177/0888325414557026, 1–21.

Boer, Roland and Li, Zhixiong (2015) Interpreting Socialism and Capitalism in China: A Dialectic of Utopia and Dystopia. *Utopian Studies* 26(2): 309–323.

Brenner, N., Theodore, N. and Peck, J. (2009) Neoliberal Urbanism: Models, Moments, Mutations. *SAIS Review* 29(1): 49–66.

Brubaker, Rogers (1996) *Nationalism Reframed: Nationhood and the National Question in the New Europe*. Cambridge: Cambridge University Press.

Brubaker, Rogers (2017) Between nationalism and civilizationism: The European populist moment in comparative perspective. *Ethnic and Racial Studies*.

Burke, Darren (2016) UKIP ditches Doncaster as venue for annual conference. Available at: www.doncasterfreepress.co.uk/news/ukip-ditches-doncaster-as-venue-for-annual-conference-1-8063848.

Butler, Judith and Athanasiou, Athena (2013) *Dispossession: The Performative in the Political*. Cambridge: Polity Press.

Campell, Chris (2018) Farage supports Donald Trump and claims Swedish city could be 'rape capital of the world'. *The Daily Express*. Available at: www.express.co.uk/news/world/769920/Nigel-Farage-Donald-Trump-Sweden-Malmo-rape. Accessed on 18 January 2018.

Carrier, James G. and Kalb, Don, eds (2015) *Anthropologies of Class: Power, Practice and Inequality*. Cambridge: Cambridge University Press.

Djuve, Anne Britt, Horgen Friberg, Jon, Tyldum, Guri and Huafeng Zhang (2015) *When poverty meets affluence: Migrants from Romania on the streets of the Scandinavian capitals*. Oslo: FAFO.

Dooley, Brian (2017) The Orban Trump bromance is complicated for both Hungary and the U.S. *Huffington Post*. Available at www.huffingtonpost.com/entry/the-orban-trump-bromance-its-complicated_us_58ebebc7e4b0145a227cb77a.

Douglas, Mary (2005) *Purity and Danger: an Analysis of Concept of Pollution and Taboo*. New York: Routledge.

Ekholm Friedman, Kajsa and Friedman, Jonathan (2008) *Historical Transformations: The Anthropology of Global Systems*. Lanham, MD: Rowman & Littlefield.

Engebrigtsen, Ada (2012) Tiggerbander og kriminelle bakmenn, eller fattige EU-borgere? *NOVA notat2*.

Eriksen, Thomas Hylland (2016) *The three crises of globalisation: An anthropological history of the early 21st century*. London: Pluto Press.

Eriksen, Thomas Hylland (2016b) *Overheating: An Anthropology of Accelerated Change*. London: Pluto.

Eriksen, Thomas Hylland and Schober, Elisabeth (2016) *Identity Destabilised: Living in an Overheated World*. Pluto Press.

Esposito, J.L. and Kalin, I. (2011) *Islamophobia: The challenge of pluralism in the 21st century*. Oxford: Oxford University Press.

References

Eurostat (2014) Government Finance Statistics. Available at: http://epp.eurostat.ec. europa.eu/portal/page/portal/government_finance_statistics/introduction. Accessed on 22 February 2014.

Fairclough, N. (2003) *Analysing Discourse: Textual Analysis for Social Research*. London: Routledge.

Fangen, Katrine (1999) On the Margins of Life: Life Stories of Radical Nationalists. *Acta Sociologica* 42: 359–363.

Farage, Nigel (2016) Pan-European Migrant Rape Story Response Highlights The Continent's Unconditional Surrender. *Breitbart News*. Available at: www.breitbart.com/london/2016/01/08/2728817/. Accessed on 4 April 2016.

Farkas, Lilla (2014) *Report on discrimination of Roma children in Education*. Brussels: European Commission.

Feischmidt, Margit and Hervik, Peter (2015) Mainstreaming the extreme: Intersecting challenges from the far right in Europe. *Intersections* 1(1): 3–17.

Foucault, Michel (2008) *The Birth of Biopolitics. Lectures at the Collège de France, 1978–1979*. Basingstoke: Palgrave Macmillan.

Fox, Jon E. (2016) The edges of the nation: A research agenda for uncovering the taken-for-granted foundations of everyday nationhood. *Nations and Nationalism*, 1–22.

Fox, Jon and Miller-Indriss, Cynthia (2008) Everyday Nationhood. *Ethnicities* 8(4): 536–562.

Fukuyama, Francis (2018) *Identity: The Demand for Dignity and the Politics of Resentment*. Farrar, Straus and Giroux.

Ganucheau, Adam (2016) How Donald Trump and Nigel Farage met in Mississippi. *Mississippi Today*, 15 November. Available at https://mississippitoday.org/2016/11/15/how-donald-trump-and-nigel-farage-met-in-mississippi/.

Geertz, Clifford (1973) *The Interpretation of Cultures*. Basic Books.

Gellner, E. (1983) *Nations and Nationalism*. Oxford: Blackwell.

Gilroy, P. (1987) *'There ain't no black in the Union Jack': The Cultural Politics of Race and Nation*. London: Hutchinson.

Gilroy, P. (2000) *Between Camps. Nations, Cultures and the Allure of Race*. London: Routledge.

Gingrich, A. and Banks, M. (2006) *Neo-Nationalism in Europe & Beyond: Perspectives from Social Anthropology*. New York: Berghahn Books.

Goodwin, M. (2011) *New British Fascism: Rise of the British National Party*. Princeton: Princeton University Press.

Goodwin, Matthew and Ford, Robert (2014) *Revolt on the right: Explaining support for the radical right in Britain*. Routledge.

Goodwin, Matthew and Heath, Oliver (2016) The 2016 referendum, Brexit and the Left Behind: An aggregate-level analysis of the result. *Political Quarterly*.

Gordin, Michael D., Tilley, Helen and Prakash, Gyan (2010) *Utopia/Dystopia: Conditions of historical possibility*. Princeton: Princeton University Press.

Gullestad, Marianne (2006) Imagined Kinship: The Role of Descent in the Rearticulation of Norwegian Ethno-Nationalism. In Andre Gingrich and Marcus Banks, eds, *Neo-Nationalism in Europe & Beyond: Perspectives from Social Anthropology*. New York: Berghahn Books, 69–91.

Hancock, Ian (2007) *We Are the Romani people*. Hertfordshire: University of Hertfordshire Press.

References

Hann, Chris (2015) *The new Völkerwanderungen: Hungary and Germany, Europe and Eurasia.* Available at: www.focaalblog.com/2015/09/11/chris-hann-the-new-volkerwanderungen-hungary-and-germany-europe-and-eurasia/. Accessed on 23 January 2015.

Helms, Elissa (2015) *Men at the borders: Gender, victimhood, and war in Europe's refugee crisis.* Available at www.focaalblog.com/2015/12/22/elissa-helms-men-at-the-borders-gender-victimhood-and-war-in-europes-refugee-crisis/#sthash.W05kSi2v.dpuf. Accessed on 15 January 2016.

Herzfeld, M. (1997) *Cultural Intimacy: Social Poetics in the Nation-State.* New York: Routledge.

Herzfeld, Michael (2016) Critical reactions: The ethnographic genealogy of response. *Social Anthropology* 24(2): 200–204.

Hinde, Dominic (2016) *A utopia like any other: Inside the Swedish Model.* Luath Press.

Hobsbawm, Eric (1991) *Nations and Nationalism since 1780: Programme, myth, reality.* Cambridge: Cambridge University Press.

Hobsbawm, E. and Ranger, T. (1983) *The Invention of Tradition.* Cambridge: Cambridge University Press.

Hochschild, Arlie (2018) *Strangers in their own land: Anger and mourning on the American right.* The New Press.

Hodges, Lucy (1997) Singular Man of Sceptical Faith. *Times Higher Education.* TES Global Ltd., 17 Apr. Web. 23 Jan. 2015.

Holmes, Douglas (2000) *Integral Europe: Fast-Capitalism, Multiculturalism, Neofascism.* Princeton, NJ: Princeton University Press.

Hübinette, Tobias (2013) Swedish Antiracism and White Melancholia: Racial Words in a Post-racial Society. *Ethnicity and Race in a Changing World* 4(1) (Autumn).

Hübinette, Tobias and Lundström, Catrin (2014) Three phases of hegemonic whiteness: Understanding racial temporalities in Sweden. *Social Identities: Journal for the Study of Race, Nation and Culture* 20(6): 423–437.

Huntington, S.P. (1996) *The Clash of Civilizations and the Remaking of World Order.* New York: Simon & Schuster.

Husøy, Eirik (2018) Sveriges statsminister utelukker ikke å sette inn militæret mot gjengkriminaliteten (The PM of Sweden does not rule out using the military against organized crime). *Aftenposten*, 18 January. Available at: www.aftenposten.no/verden/i/4dzVG6/Sveriges-statsminister-utelukker-ikke-a-sette-inn-militaret-mot-gjengkriminaliteten. Accessed on 19 January 2018.

Hutchings, Stephen (2012) The gypsy as vanishing mediator in Russian television coverage of inter-ethnic tension. *Nationalities Papers: The journal of nationalism and ethnicity* 41(6).

Infowars (2017) Sweden under pressure to adopt Islamic national flag, 14 November. Available at: www.infowars.com/sweden-under-pressure-to-adopt-islamic-national-flag/.

Ivarsflaten, Elisabeth (2008) What Unites Right-Wing Populists in Western Europe? Re-Examining Grievance Mobilization Models in Seven Successful Cases. *Comparative Political Studies* 41(1): 3–23.

Ivarsflaten, Elisabeth and Gudrandsen, Frøy (2014) The Populist Radical Right in Western Europe. In *Europa Regional Surveys of the World.* London: Routledge.

Jean-Klein, Iris (2001) Nationalism and Resistance: The Two Faces of Everyday Activism in Palestine During the Intifada. *Cultural Anthropology* 16(1): 83–126.

Jobbik (2010) *Radical Change: A Guide to Jobbik's Parliamentary Electoral Manifesto for National Self-Determination and Social Justice.* Budapest: Jobbik Foreign Affairs Committee.

References

Jupskås, Anders Ravik (2016) The taming of the shrew: how the Progress Party (almost) became part of the mainstream. In Tjitske Akkerman, Sarah De Lange and Matthijs Rooduijn, eds, *Radical right-wing populist parties in Western Europe – Into the mainstream?* Routledge.

Jurgensmeyer, Mark (2003) *Terror in the Mind of God: The Global Rise of Religious Violence.* California: University of California Press.

Kalb, Don and Halmani, Gábor (2011) *Headlines of Nation, Subtexts of Class: Working class populism and the return of the repressed in neoliberal Europe.* London: Berghahn Books.

Kassam, Raheem (2017) *No Go Zones: How Sharia law is coming to a neighborhood near you.* Regnery Publishing.

Kaufman, Eric (2017) Levels or changes? Ethnic context, immigration and the UK Independence Party vote. *Electoral Studies* 48: 57–69.

Kaufman, Eric (2018) *Whiteshift: Populism, Immigration and the Future of White Majorities.* Penguin.

Kimmel, Michael (2003) Globalization and its Mal(e)contents: The Gendered Moral and Political Economy of Terrorism. *International Sociology* 18(3): 603–620.

Knowles, Caroline (2003) *Race and Social Analysis.* Sage Publications.

Kornai, János (2015) Hungary's U-turn. *Society and Economy* 37(3): 279–329.

Kovács, András (2012) *The stranger at hand: Anti-Semitic prejudices in post-communist Hungary.* Brill.

Kovács, Mária M. (2015) Personal interview with Mária M. Kovács in Budapest.

Lakoff, George (2008) *The Political Mind: A Cognitive Scientist's Guide to Your Brain and its Politics.* Viking Press.

Mastnak, Tomaz (2002) *Crusading Peace: Christendom, the Muslim World, and Western Political Order.* Berkeley: University of California Press.

May, S., Modood, T. and Squires, J. (2004) *Ethnicity, Nationalism, and Minority Rights.* Cambridge: Cambridge University Press.

Midtbøen, Arnfinn Haagensen and Lidén, Hilde (2015) *Diskriminering av samer, nasjonale minoriteter og innvandrere i Norge. En kunnskapsgjennomgang* (Discrimination of Sami, national minorities and immigrants in Norway. An overview of extant knowledge). Rapport 2015:01. Oslo: Institutt for samfunnsforskning.

Moghadam, Valentine M., ed. (1994) *Gender and National Identity: Women and Politics in Muslim Societies.* London and New Jersey: Zed Books.

Mollona, Massimilano (2010) *Made in Sheffield: An Ethnography of Industrial Work and Politics.* London: Berghahn Books.

More, Thomas (2012) [1516] *Utopia.* NY: Dover Publications.

Mudde, C. (2004) The Populist Zeitgeist. *Government and Opposition* 39(4): 542–563.

Mudde, C. (2007) *Populist Radical Right Parties in Europe.* Cambridge: Cambridge University Press.

Mudde, C. (2009) *Populist Radical Right Parties in Europe.* Cambridge: Cambridge University Press.

Mudde, Cas (2017) *The far right in America.* London: Routledge.

Mudde, Cas and Kaltwasser, Cristobal (2017) *Populism: A very short introduction.* Oxford University Press.

Muehlebach, Andrea and Shoshan, Nitzan (2012) Post-Fordist Affect: Introduction. *Anthropological Quarterly* 85(2): 317–343.

Müller, J.-W. (2016) *What is Populism?* University of Pennsylvania Press.

Nagel, Joane (2010) Masculinity and nationalism: Gender and sexuality in the making of nations. *Ethnic and Racial Studies* 21(2): 242–269.

Norris, Pippa and Inglehart, Ronald (2016) *Trump, Brexit, and the Rise of Populism: Economic Have-Nots and Cultural Backlash.* KS Working Paper No. RWP16-026.

Norwegian Broadcasting Corporation (NRK) (2012) Frp-leder Siv Jensen frykter tiggerboom i Norge til sommeren [Progress Party leader Siv Jensen fear begging boom in Norway this summer]. Available at: www.nrk.no/norge/jensen_-_-nok-er-nok_-senddem-ut-1.8244413.

Odone, Christina (2013) Nigel Farage: We Must Defend Christian Heritage. *The Telegraph*, 1 Nov. Web. 26 Mar. 2015.

Office for National Statistics (ONS) (2003) *Local Authority Profiles & Population Pyramids: Yorkshire and the Humber. Census 2001.* Available at: www.ons.gov.uk/ons/rel/census/census-2001-local-authorityprofiles/local-authority-profiles/index.html.

Okely, J. (1983) *The Traveller-Gypsies.* Cambridge: Cambridge University Press.

Pauwels, T. (2011) Measuring populism: A quantitative text analysis of party literature in Belgium. *Journal of Elections, Public Opinion and Parties* 21(1): 97–119.

Pelkmans, Mathijs (2006) *Defending the border: Identity, religion, and modernity in the Republic of Georgia.* Ithaca and London: Cornell University Press.

Pickering, Michael and Keightley, Emily (2006) The Modalities of Nostalgia. *Current Sociology* 54(6): 919–941.

Piketty, Thomas (2014) *Capital in the Twenty-First Century.* London: Belknap Press.

Pirro, Andrea (2014) *The Populist Radical Right in Central and Eastern Europe: Ideology, impact and electoral performance.* London: Routledge.

Prime Minister's Office (2015a) National consultation on immigration to begin, 24 April. Available at www.kormany.hu/en/prime-minister-s-office/news/national-consultation-on-immigration-to-begin.

Prime Minister's Office (2015b) Prime Minister Viktor Orbán's address to Parliament before the start of daily business, 21 September. Available at www.kormany.hu/en/the-prime-minister/the-prime-minister-s-speeches/prime-minister-viktor-orban-s-addredss-to-parliament-before-the-start-of-daily-business.

Rachod-Nilsson, Sita and Tetrault, Mary Ann (2003) *Women, States and Nationalism: At Home in the Nation?* London: Routledge.

Rooduijn, Matthijs (2014) The Mesmerising Message: The Diffusion of Populism in Public Debates in Western European Media. *Political Studies* 62(4).

Rooduijn, M. and Pauwels, T. (2011) Measuring Populism: Comparing Two Methods of Content Analysis. *West European Politics* 34(6): 1272–1283.

Rudgren, Jens and Ruth, Patric (2013) Contextual explanations of radical right-wing support in Sweden: Socioeconomic marginalization, group threat, and the halo effect. *Ethnic and Racial Studies* 36(4).

Sassen, Saskia (2007) *Deciphering the Global: Its Spaces, Scales and Subjects.* Routledge.

Schiff, András (2013) Hungarians must face Nazi past not venerate it. *The Guardian.* Available at: www.theguardian.com/commentisfree/2013/dec/11/hungarians-must-face-nazi-past-not-venerate-it.

Schober, Elisabeth (2016) *Base Encounters: The US Armed Forces in South Korea.* Pluto Press.

Skey, Michael (2011) *National Belonging and Everyday Life: The Significance of Nationhood in an Uncertain World.* Palgrave Macmillan.

References

Smith, Anthony (1999) *Myths and Memories of the Nation*. Oxford: Oxford University Press.
Smith, A. (2003) *Chosen Peoples: Sacred Sources of National Identity*. Oxford University Press.
Standing, Guy (2014) *The precariat: The new dangerous class*. London: Bloomsbury.
Stellings, Laurence (2015) The UKIP Index: Who's Voting UKIP? *Populus*, 12 Feb. Web. 27 Mar. 2015.
Stewart, Michael, ed. (2012) *The Gypsy 'Menace': Populism and the new anti-gypsy politics*. London: Hurst and Company.
Stolcke, V. (1995) Talking Culture: New Boundaries, New Rhetorics of Exclusion in Europe. *Current Anthropology* 36(1): 1–24.
Stolz, J. (2005) Explaining Islamophobia. A test of four theories based on the case of a Swiss city. *Swiss Journal of Sociology* 31: 547–566.
Strathern, Marilyn (1995) Nostalgia and the New Genetics. In D. Battaglia, ed., *Rhetorics of Self-Making*. Berkeley: University of California Press.
The Swedish Government (2017) *Facts about migration, integration and crime in Sweden*. Available at www.government.se/articles/2017/02/facts-about-migration-and-crime-in-sweden/. Accessed on 11 January 2018.
Taggart, Paul (2004) Populism and Representative Politics in Contemporary Europe. *Journal of Political Ideologies* 9(3).
Tambiah, Stanley (1990) Presidential Address: Reflections on Communal Violence in South Asia. *Journal of Asian Studies* 49(4).
Taylor, Charles (2004) *Modern Social Imaginaries*. Durham, NC: Duke University Press.
Teitelbaum, Jonathan (2017) *Lions of the North: Sounds of the new Nordic radical nationalism*. Oxford: Oxford University Press.
Thorleifsson, Cathrine (2017) Disposable Strangers: Far right securitisation of migration in Hungary. *Social Anthropology* 25(3): 318–334.
Trump, Donald (2016) Twitter message, 9 November 2016.
Tuffrey, Peter (2011) *Doncaster's Collieries*. Gloucestershire: Amberley Publishing.
Twine, F.W. and Gallagher, C. (2008) The future of whiteness: A map of the 'third wave'. *Ethnic and Racial Studies* 31(1): 4–24.
Ukip (2015) *Ukip Manifesto 2015*. Ukip.org. 1 Jan. 2015. Web. 19 Apr. 2015.
Urbinati, N. (2014) *Democracy disfigured. Opinion, truth, and the people*. Cambridge, Mass: Harvard University Press.
Van Kessel, Stijn (2011) Explaining the Electoral Performance of Populist Parties: The Netherlands as a Case Study. *Perspectives on European Politics and Society* 12(1).
Vermeersch, Peter (2006) *The Romani Movement: Minority Politics and Ethnic Mobilization in Contemporary Central Europe*. New York: Berghahn Books.
Vertovec, Stephen (2007) Super-Diversity and its Implications. *Ethnic and Racial Studies* 30(6): 1024–1054.
Vetlesen, A.J. (2005) *Evil and Human Agency: Understanding Collective Evildoing*. Cambridge University Press.
Vidra, Zs. and Fox, J. (2014) Mainstreaming of Racist Anti-Roma Discourses in the Media in Hungary. *Journal of Immigrant and Refugee Studies* 12(4): 437–455.
Visvanathan, Shiv (2014) Rethinking Waste: Time, Obsolescence, Diversity and Democracy. In Raminder Kaur and Parul Dave-Mukherji, eds, *Arts and Aesthetics in a Globalizing World*.

Vona, Gábor (2012) *Született augusztus 20-án* [Born on 20 August]. Hungary: Magyar Hirek.Kft.

Wadsworth, Jonathan et al. (2016) Immigration from the EU is not a 'necessary evil' and does not drag down wages. *LSE blogs*. Available at http://blogs.lse.ac.uk/brexit/2016/05/11/immigration-from-the-eu-is-not-a-necessary-evil-and-does-not-drag-down-wages/.

Weiss-Wendt, Anton, ed. (2013) *The Nazi Genocide of the Roma: Reassessment and Commemoration*. London: Berghahn.

Wodak, Ruth (2015) *The politics of fear: What right-wing populist discourse means*. London: Sage.

Wodak, R., de Cillia, R., Reisigl, M. and Liebhart, K. (1999) *The Discursive Construction of National Identity*. Edinburgh: Edinburgh University Press.

Yuval-Davis, Nira (1997) *Gender and Nation*. London: Sage Publications.

Index

AFD (Alternative for Germany) party 1
Agamben, Giorgio 48
Åkesson, Jimmi 80
alt-right 41
anti-semitism *see* Jews and anti-semitism
antiziganism *see* Roma and antiziganism
Arendt, Hannah 48
assimilation 8, 77, 89–90, 94
Aston, Guy 25, 37
asylum seekers *see* refugee crisis of 2015
Austrian Freedom Party (FPÖ) 1
authenticity 2, 9, 27, 33, 41, 45, 80
authoritarianism 1–2, 87, 102–3

Bachman, Michele 41
Banks, M. 6
Bannon, Stephen 40–2, 69
Barth, Fredrik 7
Bauman, Zygmunt 10, 47, 51, 60, 62, 72
begging 91–3, 95, 99
Belgium, terrorist attacks in 53, 82
belonging 2, 8, 11, 27, 29, 32, 46, 103
biological weapon, Muslims as Jews' 57–8, 78
Blaycock, Ian 21
Boer, Roland 75–6
borders: border-crossing, act of 48, 70; closure 48; control 56–8, 61–2, 84; Hungary 56–8, 61–2, 84; open borders 57–8; symbolic borders 22
boundaries of the nation 3, 5–7, 10, 44, 48, 68, 73, 88
Bozó, István 66
branding 19–22, 37, 41, 61
'Breaking Point' poster 43–4, 69
Breibart News 35, 40–2, 78, 83
Breivik, Anders Behring 86
Brexit: 'Breaking Point' poster 43–4, 69; class divisions 44; establishment and elites 44; freedom of movement 39; Leave campaign 37; referendum 103; refugee crisis 45–6; regional divisions 44; Ukip 22, 23–4, 30–2, 36–46, 69, 101, 103; xenophobia 103; wages, effect on 23; white supremacy 45; working class 44–5
Britain First 34–5
Britishness 27–8, 29, 83
Brubaker, Rogers 7
Budapest, Hungary 7, 63, 65–7, 70
Bulgaria 89

Cameron, David 34
Carlson, Tucker 77
casualization 15
Central Asia, conflicts in 49
Charlottesville, United States, demonstration in 36
children, sexual grooming of 43
Christian civilization, threats to *see* civilization, threats to
Church City Mission, Oslo 95
civic nationalism 37, 45
civilization: Brexit 42, 44–5; clash of civilizations 44, 51; human waste 47; Hungary 2, 8, 42, 52–3, 57, 66–8; Muslim migrants 8, 10, 42, 44, 52–3, 57, 66–8, 76, 81–2, 102; Roma 99; Sweden 75–6, 81–2, 87–8, 102; Ukip 10, 27–8, 35, 42–6, 82; whiteness 35, 44
class: Brexit 44; Hungary 9, 60–1; middle class 9, 60–1 *see also* working/lower class
climate change denial 31–2
Clinton, Hillary 44
coal nationalism: affect factory, mining as 13; climate change denial 31–2;

114   Index

closures of pits 12–13, 17–18, 21–2; Doncaster 11–13, 17–22, 29–33, 101; heritage, restoring 20; identity and dignity 13; nostalgia 17–18, 29–30; precarity 14–15; Ukip 11, 22
Coalfield Communities Campaign 13
Cologne, Germany, on New Year's Eve, sexual assaults in 42–3
colonialism 28–9, 43, 45
Commonwealth 15
communication channels 5–6, 34, 41 *see also* social media
competition 8, 12–13, 23, 27, 31–2, 59–60, 91
conspiracy theories 57–8, 73, 78, 102
cosmopolitanism 26, 29–31, 87
crimmigrants: dystopian imaginaries 8–9; Hungary 62–7, 84; Muslim migrants 8–10, 47, 52, 62–7, 72, 102; *rapefugees* 79, 84; refugee crisis of 2015 10, 47, 52, 62–7, 72, 102; sexual violence 79, 84; Sweden 79, 82–4, 87; Trump campaign 41; Ukip 41–6; violent imaginaries 42–4, 46
Cromwell, Oliver 26
culture 3–4, 6, 8–10, 103; Hungary 8, 60, 66–7, 72, 86; identity 1–2, 101; multiculturalism 15, 36, 61, 76, 81–2, 87; Muslim migrants 46; nature divide 91, 100; Norway 8; Roma 91, 99–100; Sweden 77, 81; Ukip 10, 27, 29–30, 32, 45, 101; values 47

dehumanization 10, 47, 69, 90, 100
demand side 6–7
demographic change: Hungary 67–8, 78; overheating effect 4, 8; Ukip 8, 15, 22, 24, 59, 80–1, 101
displacement 78, 104; colonialism 28; Islamophobia 42; refugee crisis of 2015 44, 48–9, 51–2, 66, 72–3; terrorism 45, 84
diversification 1, 3–5, 11–12, 15, 23, 29–33, 45
Doncaster, England, Ukip supporters in 7–8, 11–33; branding into the future 19–22; coal nationalism 11–13, 17–22, 29–33, 101; cosmopolitanism 29–31; culture 10, 27, 29–30, 32, 45, 101; demographic change 8, 15, 22, 24, 59, 101; diversification 11–12, 15, 23, 29–33, 45; economic insecurities 8, 17, 19–25, 32–3, 101; Eastern European migrants 8, 15, 22, 23–5, 28–9, 101; ethnicity 10, 11, 15, 25–7, 29–33; EU/Brexit 22, 23–4, 30–2, 44–5, 101; fear, politics of 11, 26–8, 33; Fordism 11, 12–13, 19; global economic crisis of 2008 8, 12, 14; identity 15–19, 25–7, 30, 32–3, 101; Labour Party 11, 22, 23–4, 38; migrants and minorities 10, 11, 22–9, 32–3, 101; Muslim migrants 10, 27–8; myths 24, 26; neoliberal restructuring of economy 11–15, 32; nostalgia 11, 15–19, 22, 25, 27–31, 33; older people 18, 21–8; overheating 8, 11–12; party conferences 37–40, 79–80; precarity 11, 13–15, 19, 32–3, 101; racism 24–5, 27, 30–1, 34–6; Roma and travellers 15, 91; Roman roots 21–2; Sikh minority 27–9; socio-economic inequality 12, 15; Swedish dystopia, use of 75, 79–80; training 34–5; unemployment 11, 13, 14, 17, 23; whiteness 10, 11, 15, 27, 29–30, 33; working class 8, 11–29, 33, 36; young persons 29–31
Doncaster Free Press 37
Doncaster Gazette 13
Doncaster Star 13
Doncopolitan 29
Douglas, Mary 48
Draper, Warren 29
Dublin Refugee Convention 51
Duke, David 35–6
Dúró, Dóra 61
Dutch Party for Freedom (PVV) 40
dystopia 8–9, 41–2, 52, 54 *see also* Swedish dystopian and violent imaginaries

East Central Europe, Muslims in 49
Eastern Europe 8, 15, 22, 23–5, 28–9, 48–9, 101
economic insecurities 3–4; globalization 1, 3; Hungary 8, 10, 47, 51–2, 58–60, 101–2; hyperinstrumentalization of migrants as economic threat 10, 47; refugee crisis of 2015 51–2, 58–60, 101–2; Roma 90; Sweden 3, 8; Ukip 8, 17, 19–25, 32–3, 101
educational level 8, 9, 14, 33, 44, 60, 80
Edward I, King of England 19
electoral campaigns: European Parliament elections 2014 80; Hungary 2, 50, 53–5, 58–65, 69–72; Norway 83–4; refugee crisis of 2015 50, 53, 58, 62, 69–70; Ukip 22, 26, 80;

xenophobia 2, 22, 34, 58, 69 *see also* Trump presidential campaign
elites *see* establishment and elites
end of history 3
enemies of the nation 10, 41–2, 47, 60–2
England 4; Britishness 27–8, 29; Englishness 26–8, 29, 31–2, 37, 46; whiteness 37 *see also* Doncaster, England, Ukip supporters in; United Kingdom
English Democrats 26
Eriksen, Thomas Hylland 4
essentialism 9, 41, 45, 82
establishment and elites: EU 44, 51; Hungary 86; Norway 83; pure nation versus corrupt elite 2–3; Sweden 80, 86–7; traitors, liberal establishment as 86–7; Trump campaign 41, 44–5; Ukip 26, 41, 43–5, 80, 101
ethnicity: boundaries 7; Hungary 1, 5, 8, 50, 68–70; nationalism 1, 5, 8, 49–50, 68–70; nationhood 47; Sweden 75; Ukip 10, 11, 15, 25–7, 29–33, 35 *see also* racism and xenophobia; whiteness
ethnography 6–8
Euroabia 78
Europe of Freedom and Direct Democracy grouping in European Parliament 80
European Union: European Parliament elections 2014 80; Euroscepticism 1, 26–7, 31; freedom of movement 38–9, 83, 89, 93–4; Hungary 50, 51–2, 59, 68, 70, 72, 103; myths 26; Norway 40; refugee crisis of 2015 50, 51–2, 68, 70, 72; regeneration 13; Roma 89, 93–4; Schengen area 59, 89; Sweden 83; Turkey joining EU, prospect of 82; Ukip 22, 23–7, 30–2, 44–5, 101, 103 *see also* Brexit
Evangelical Contact Centre, Oslo 94–5
everyday life 2, 6–7, 10, 23, 54
evictions 92, 96–9
exception *see* human waste/exception populations
exceptionalism 81
exclusion 2, 8, 10–11, 49, 89–90

Facebook 5–6, 34, 56, 59–60
falsification of history 70–1
families 68

Index 115

Farage, Nigel 22, 33, 34–5, 37–40, 42–5, 78–9
fascism 1, 9, 29, 35–6, 60
fear, politics of 8; Hungary 51–3, 58–60, 63, 65, 69–70, 84; migrants and minorities 51–3, 58–60, 65, 69–70, 102–3; Norway 83–4; refugee crisis of 2015 51–3, 58–60, 65, 69–70; Sweden 83–4; Turkey joining EU, prospect of 82; Ukip 11, 26–8, 33, 41–3, 45
feminism 5
fence, construction of a 53, 61, 84
Fico, Robert 49
Fidesz (Hungary) 1, 5, 47–74, 102–3; anti-semitism 58; awareness campaign 51; 'Breaking Point' poster 69; Christian civilization, threats to 8, 52, 68; cultural insecurities 8, 60; economic insecurities 8, 60; election campaign 2018 2, 58–65, 69–72; ethnic nationalism 1, 5, 8, 50; EU 103; fear, politics of 53, 58–9, 63, 65, 70; fence, construction of a razor-wire 53, 61, 84; gender roles and nuclear family 68; Islamophobia 58, 102; Jobbik 50, 53, 58, 61–3, 65, 69–73, 84, 102; Muslim migrants 8, 47–74; origins 50; refugee crisis of 2015 8, 10, 47–74; securitization 56, 60, 67 ; Sweden 84; xenophobia 2, 53, 65
Fordism 11, 12–13, 19
FPÖ (Austrian Freedom Party) 1
France: Jews, attacks on 53; Paris, terrorist atrocities in 51; presidential elections 1
Fransen, Jayda 35
Freedom 70
Front National (France) 53
Frontex 70
Fukuyama, Francis 3

Geertz, Clifford 7
gender 5, 7; Hungary 65, 68, 85–7; masculinity 3, 36, 43, 85–7; Other 79; resentment 3; traditional roles 68; Ukip 34; white masculinity 85–7 *see also* women
generational differences: Hungary 9, 60–1; older people 18, 21–8; Ukip 18, 21–31; young people 9, 29–31, 60–1
Georgina, Bernáth 61

Germany: Cologne on New Year's Eve, sexual assaults in 42–3; Hungary 42–3; refugee crisis of 2015 48
Gibson, Mel 19
Gill, John 34–5, 38
Gingrich, A. 6
global economic crisis of 2008 8, 12, 14, 58–9
globalization: crisis of globalization 4, 5, 75 ; dystopia 75; economic insecurities 1, 3; human waste/exception populations 47; inequalities 4; Islamophobia 102; losers of globalization 3; Muslim migrants 58, 75, 102; neoliberal restructuring of economy 32; open borders 57–8; precarity of labour 14–15
Gordin, Michael D. 75–6
Gorka, Sebastian 68–9
grammars of exclusion 5–6, 10, 101–2; Brexit 44–5; Hungary 47, 53–9, 65, 69, 72; Sweden 87; Trump campaign 44–5
Gran, Kari 95–6
Gregor, Bernadett 66
grievances 8–9, 22, 45, 101–3
grooming 43
Gyöngyösi, Márton 54, 65
Gyurcsány, Ferenc 58

Halmani, Gábor 6
Hatfield Colliery, Doncaster 15
Hauger, Jan 96–7
health 96–9
Hegedüs Jr, Lóránt 66
Helmer, Roger 31–2, 37
Helsinki Committee 70
heritage 10, 20, 31, 35, 40, 42–5
Hitler, Adolf 60, 66
Holmes, Douglas 6
Holocaust 70–1, 90
Hookem, Mike 40
Horthy, Miklós 65–6
human waste/exception populations: dehumanization 47; dirt 48; economic lines, disposable on 47; gender lines, disposable on 47; Hungary 10, 47–8, 51–3, 56–7, 60, 70, 72–3; Muslim migrants 2, 10, 47, 51–3, 60, 66; racial lines, disposable on 47; refugee crisis of 2015 10, 47–8, 51–3, 56–7, 60, 66, 70–3; Roma 10, 90, 96–100
Hungary 1=2, 4; civilization, threats to 2, 8, 42, 52–3, 57, 66–8; establishment and elites 86; EU 59, 103; Greater Hungary 60, 63, 66; Holocaust memorial 70–1; illiberal state, Hungary as 50, 61, 68, 72–3, 103; rhetoric 53–4, 57–8, 61, 65, 102; transit country, Hungary as a 49–50; vigilantes 87 *see also* Fidesz (Hungary); Jobbik (Hungary)

hyperinstrumentalization of migrants as economic threat 10, 47
hypermasculinity 43

identity: affirmation of identity 3; borders, symbolic and physical 22; coal nationalism 13; culture 101; diversification 15; Hungary 8, 61, 73; national identity 9–12, 61, 75–6, 86, 97–8, 102; overheating effect 8–9, 49; politics 4, 104; racialization 46; Roma 90–1, 94; Ukip 8, 15–19, 25–7, 30, 32–3, 101
illiberal state 50, 61, 68, 72–3, 103
imaginaries 2, 5; communities 73, 89, 94; enemies 60–2; Other 104; social imaginaries 76; violent imaginaries 10, 35, 42–7, 57, 65, 75–88
immigration *see* migrants and minorities
industrialism 8, 17, 32; coal nationalism 11–13, 17–18, 21–2, 31–3, 101; past, glorifying/nostalgia for industrial 12, 19–22, 29, 31, 33; tourism 21; UK national identity 12
inequality 4, 12, 15, 78, 104
innovation 30
irredentism 50, 65–6
Irving, David 66
Islam *see* Islamophobia; Muslim migrants
Islamophobia: anti-semitism, fusing with 57–8; Brexit 42–3; globalization 102; Hungary 56–8, 69, 73, 84–5, 102; Norway 35; refugee crisis of 2015 2, 49; Sweden 78; Ukip 42–5
Israel 53

Janiczak, David 55
Jensen, Siv 92
Jews and anti-semitism: accusations, racist tropes and persecution 103; anti-Zionism 53–4, 56; Belgium, attacks in 53; biological weapon,

Muslims as Jews' 57–8, 78; conspiracy theories 57–8, 102; France, attacks in 53; Holocaust 70–1; Hungary 50, 53–4, 56–8, 61–2, 66, 69–71, 102; Islamists, attacks by 53; Islamophobia, fusing with 57–8; new anti-semitism 53; Sweden 77
Jobbik (Hungary) 1, 5, 8–9; anti-semitism 50, 53–4, 56–8, 61–2, 66, 69–70, 102; border control 56–8, 61–2, 84; branding 61; crimmigrants 10, 47, 52, 62–7, 72, 84, 102; culture 8, 60, 66–7, 72, 86; economic insecurities 8, 10, 47, 51–2, 58–60, 101–2; elections 50, 53–5, 58, 62, 69–70; ethnic nationalism 5, 50, 68–70; EU 50, 51–2, 68, 70, 72; fear, politics of 51–3, 58–60, 65, 69–70, 84; Fidesz 50, 53, 58, 61–3, 65, 69–73, 84, 102; flag, myths and symbols 60; identity 8, 61, 73; Islamophobia 56–8, 69, 73, 84–5, 102; media 61–2; Muslim migrants 47–74; Palestine, as being pro 53–4; protestors 70–2; racialization 47, 67, 73, 87, 102; rally 62–7; refugee crisis of 2015 8, 10, 47–74; Roma and antiziganism 50, 54–6, 58, 69–70, 90–1; securitization 10, 47–52, 56, 58–60, 70, 72–3, 84; social media 59–60, 70; Sweden 75, 78, 84–7; torchlight processions 85; undercover campaign on migration 62–7, 84; violence 9, 57, 65, 84–7; white masculinity 85–7; white nationalism 9, 67–9; young people 9, 60–1
József, Kalapács 85
Judeo-Christian heritage 10, 42–6, 52, 75, 79

Kaczynski, Jaroslaw 103
Kalb, Don 6
Kaltwasser, Cristobal 2
Karácsony, Gergely 58
Kárpát, Dániel 61–6, 70, 84–5
Kassam, Raheem 40–2, 78, 83
Keynesianism 13
Ku Klux Klan (KKK) 35
kuruck.info 86

labour: casualization 15; low-skilled jobs, competition over 8, 23, 27, 59; precarity 11, 13–15, 19, 32–3, 101
Labour Party 11, 22, 23–4, 38

Law and Justice Party (PiS) 49
Le Pen, Marine 1–2
left-wing anti-austerity populist parties 3
Leirstein, Ulf 92
Lenin, V.I. 41
Li, Zhixiong 75–6
liberal democracies: challenging liberal democracies 1, 6, 50, 62, 69, 103; end of history 3; enemy, as 62; illiberal states 50, 61, 68, 72–3, 103; Islamophobia 49
Listhaug, Sylvi 83
litter and pollution 96–100, 102
Löfven, Stefan 78
London 15, 26
Ludvigsen, Stian 94–5
Lundgren, Peter 80

mainstreaming 35, 38, 80
Major, John 33
'Make America great again' 36
Malmö, Sweden 78–9
Martonvásár, Hungary 7, 57, 59, 62–9
masculinity 3, 36, 43, 85–7
material conditions 1, 3–4, 8, 101
media 5, 34–5, 61–2, 96
Merkel, Angela 50, 68
Mexicans, slurs on 42
middle class 9, 60–1
Middle East, conflicts in 49
Migration Aid 70
migrants and minorities 1–7; Commonwealth 15; fear, politics of 102–3; Hungary 62–7, 84; mass immigration 4, 47, 66; myths 4–5, 24, 72, 77–8, 83–4; Norway 83; pollutants, migrants as 56–7, 72, 96–100, 102; rhetoric 42, 49, 57–8, 61, 65, 84; Sweden 10, 75–83; Ukip 10, 11, 22–9, 32–3, 36–45, 101; wages, effect on 23 *see also* crimmigrants; Muslim migrants; refugee crisis of 2015; Roma minorities in Norway
Miliband, Ed 38
Mill, John Stuart 76
Miner's Strike of 1984-85 13, 21–2
minorities *see* migrants and minorities
Molenbeek, Sweden 81–2
Molnar, Tamas 69
moral panic 52, 76
More, Thomas 76
Morgan, Piers 35
Møtestedet (Meeting Place), Oslo 95–6
Mudde, Cas 2

multiculturalism 15, 36, 61, 76, 81–2, 87
Muslim migrants: accusations, racist tropes and persecution 103; biological weapon, Muslims as Jews' 57–8, 78; civilization, threats to 8, 10, 42, 44, 52–3, 57, 66–8, 76, 81–2, 102; Cologne on New Year's Eve, sexual assaults in 42–3; globalization 58, 75, 102; human waste/exception populations 2, 10, 47, 51–3, 60, 66; Hungary 8, 56–8, 69, 73, 84–5, 102; Islamification 53, 78–9; Islamists 53; Islamization 58, 102; Other 2, 46; raperefugees 42, 79, 84; rhetoric 57–8, 61, 65, 102; Sharia law 78, 87; Sikhs 27; Sweden 75–80, 81–2; terrorism 42, 45, 51–2, 56, 63–8, 76, 82–7; Ukip 10, 27–8, 35–6, 42–4, 46, 80; United States, ban on entry to 36, 42; war on radical Islam 42; women, status of 81 *see also* Islamophobia; refugee crisis of 2015
myths: EU 26; Hungary 60, 72; migrants and minorities 4–5, 24, 72, 77–8, 83–4; Roma 54, 90, 92, 95; Sweden 77–8, 83–4; Ukip 24, 26

National Coal Board (NCB) 12
national identity 9–12, 61, 75–6, 86, 97–8, 102
nationhood 47, 73, 87
nature 89–91, 97–100, 102
nativism 10, 36, 44–6, 50, 80

Nazi-dominated Europe 90
neoliberal restructuring of economy 3, 11–15, 32, 60
Nesvik, Harald Tom 92
New Labour 22
no-go zones 78, 83–4, 87
North Africa, conflicts in 49
Norway 4–6; fear, politics of 83–4; general election 2017 83; No the EU movement 40; social media 5–6; terrorism 86 *see also* Progress Party (Norway); Roma minorities in Norway
nostalgia 3, 102–3; coal nationalism 17–18, 29–30; cultural stereotypes 15; Fordism 19; Hungary 8; identity 15, 17; religious identities, rediscovery of 15; Sikhs 27–8; structural nostalgia 22; Sweden 77; Ukip 8, 11, 15–19, 22, 25, 27–31, 33

Novák, Előd 61
Nuttall, Paul 80–2

opposition and resistance 70–2
Orbán, Viktor 1–2, 50–4, 58–9, 65, 67–72, 84, 86, 102–3
organized crime 78, 92–3, 100
Orientalism 43
Oslo, Norway 7, 89–100, 93–4
Other: colonialism 45; dispossession 77; Hungary 10, 47, 49–59, 66, 69, 72, 102; imaginaries 104; male Other 79; Muslim migrants 2, 46; protectionism 58–60; racism 37; refugee crisis of 2015 10, 47, 49–59, 66, 69, 72, 102; Roma 88, 90, 98–9; Sweden 10, 77, 79, 102; Trump campaign 102; Ukip 102
overheating effect: Brexit 44; cooling off 12; definition 4; identity 8–9, 49; multiscalar overheating 11–12; recognition 8–9; Ukip 8, 11–12
Ózd, Hungary 7, 54–5, 57, 59

Palestine 53–4
Palin, Sarah 41
Paris, terrorist atrocities in 51
Pentecostal movement 94–5
pit closures 12–13, 17–18, 21–2
Poland 15–16, 23–4, 28–9, 49, 101, 103
political correctness 36, 43, 80–1
pollutants, migrants as 56–7, 72, 96–100, 102
populism, definition of 2–3
post-industrial towns 8 *see also* Doncaster, England, Ukip supporters in
poverty 13, 19, 23, 57, 59, 78, 82, 89, 94–9

precarity: casualization 15; coal industry 14–15; globalization 14–15; labour, of 11, 13–15, 19, 32–3, 101; refugee crisis of 2015 51, 58–60; Roma 90, 93–4, 96–7, 99–100; Ukip 11, 13–15, 19, 32–3, 101
presidential campaign *see* Trump presidential campaign
processions and protests: Hungary 70–2, 85; refugee crisis of 2015 70–2
Progress Party (Norway) 1, 5; economic insecurities 3; election campaign of 2017 83–4; global economic crisis of

2008 8; Islamophobia 35; migrants and minorities 83; Norwegian-ness, dominant ideas of 8; right, pushing politics to the 103; Roma 90–1, 98, 100, 102; Sweden 75
protectionism 3, 4, 8, 28–9, 33, 41, 58–60
protests *see* processions and protests
purity 2–3, 6, 45; bio-social 35; multiculturalism 87; Norway 90; Sweden 77, 82, 84, 87–8

racism and xenophobia: Brexit 103; electoral campaigns 2, 22, 34, 58, 69; Hungary 47, 50–3, 62, 65, 67, 70, 73, 87, 102–3; imaginaries 10, 47; Muslim migrants 49; new racism 37; racialization 45–7, 67, 73, 87, 102; refugee crisis of 2015 47, 52–3, 62, 65, 67, 70, 73; Roma 90, 93; scientific racism 77; social problems 37; Sweden 77, 87; Trump campaign 35–6, 103; Ukip 24–5, 27, 30–1, 34–40, 45–6 *see also* Islamophobia; Jews and anti-semitism; Roma and antiziganism; whiteness
radicals 4, 9, 45
rapefugees 42, 79, 84
recognition 1, 3, 8, 27, 32, 101, 104
refugee crisis of 2015 2, 47–74; border-crossing, act of 48, 70; 'Breaking Point' poster 43–4, 69; Brexit 45–6; civic engagement 70–2; crimmigrants 10, 47, 52, 62–7, 72, 102; economic threat, migrants as 10, 47, 51–2, 58–60, 101–2; human waste 10, 47–8, 51–3, 56–7, 60, 66, 70–3; Hungary 8, 10, 47–74; hyperinstrumentalization of migrants as economic threat 10, 47; Middle East, North Africa and Central Asia, conflicts in 49; Other 10, 47, 49–59, 66, 69, 72, 102; pollutants, migrants as 56–7, 72; precarity 51, 58–60; quota proposal, rejection of 50, 56, 61, 72, 84; racialization 47, 67, 73; securitization 10, 47–52, 56, 58–60, 70, 72–3, 84;
Sweden 87; terrorism 51–2, 67–8; xenophobia 47, 49, 52–3, 62, 65, 70
regeneration 13–14
regional divisions 9, 44
re-imagination, re-narration and re-invention 2, 5, 47, 77

religion: ethno-religious values 47; Judeo-Christian heritage 10, 42–6, 52, 75, 79; Pentecostal movement 94–5; Sikhs 27–9, 46; Ukip 10, 35 *see also* civilization, threats to; Muslim migrants
rhetoric 2, 102–4; Hungary 53–4, 57–8, 61, 65, 102; migrants and minorities 42, 49, 57–8, 61, 65, 84; Muslim migrants 57–8, 61, 65, 102; Roma 92; Sweden 76, 84; Ukip 42, 49
ridicule 34
right, pushing politics to the 103
Rinkeby, Sweden 83–4
Roma and antiziganism: accusations, racist tropes and persecution 103; civilization, threats to 99; Doncaster, England 15, 91; Hungary 50, 54–6, 58, 69–70; myths 54, 90, 92, 95; past atrocities 70; stereotyping 56; Sweden 77; unemployment 54–5 *see also* Roma minorities in Norway
Roma minorities in Norway 89–100; assimilation 94; begging 91–3, 95, 99; camps 92, 96–9; Conservative Party 91; crimes against Roma 90; culture 91, 99–100; dehumanization 90; disturbance, Roma as 98–9; EU 89, 93–4; excess and expulsion 96–9; exclusion 89–90; forced evictions 92, 96–9; health 96–9; human waste 10, 90, 96–100; identity 90–1, 94; itinerant Roma 89–100; litter and pollution 96–100, 102; myths 90, 92, 95; national identity 97–8, 102; nature 89–91, 97–100, 102; organised crime 92–3, 100; Other 88, 90, 98–9; precarity 90, 93–4, 96–7, 99–100; Progress Party 90–1, 98, 100, 102; relief services 91–2, 94–5; securitization 91–3, 102; social media 92; socially dangerous, as 90, 99; stereotyping 92–3; violence 102
Romania 89, 93–4
Rotherham, England, child sexual grooming by men of Pakistani origin in 43
Rusken 96–7
rust belt 41

sameness/homogeneity 2–4, 25, 40, 47, 77, 81–3, 88, 101
Sami people 77
scapegoating 45, 51, 53–4, 60

Schengen area 59, 89
Schober, Elisabeth 76
security/securitization: Hungary 10, 47–52, 56–60, 67, 70–3, 84; precarity 19; refugee crisis of 2015 10, 47–52, 56, 58–60, 70, 72–3, 84; Roma 91–3, 102; Sweden 75, 87–8
sexual assaults 42–3, 79, 84
sexual grooming 43
Sharia law 78, 87
Sikhs 27–9, 46
silent majority 41, 44–5
Sixty-four Counties Youth Movement (HVIM) (Hungary) 65–6
Sked, Alan 26
Slovakia, Smer-SD party in 49
Smith, Adam 17
social conservatism 22, 23, 44
social media: Facebook 5–6, 34, 56, 59–60; Hungary 59–60, 70; opposition and resistance 70; Roma 92; Trump campaign 41; Ukip 41
socio-economic inequality 4, 12, 15, 78, 104
solidarity 19, 70, 72, 94
Soros, George 57–8, 62, 102
sovereign debt crisis 3
Søviknes, Terje 35
Statsbygg 98–9
Stenersen, Aina 92
stereotyping 56, 92–3
Story, Tony 21
supply side 5, 7
Sweden *see* Sweden Democrats; Swedish dystopian and violent imaginaries
Swedish dystopian and violent imaginaries 10, 75–88; boundaries, defending 88; civilization, threats to 75–6, 81–2, 87–8, 102; conditions in Sweden 77–9; crimmigrants 79, 82–4, 87; culture 77, 81; danger, protection of a nation in 83–5; dystopia, definition of 76; election campaigns 80; establishment and elites 80, 86–7; EU, exit from 83; exceptionalism 81; fear, politics of 83–4; focalization, process of 76, 87; home, epitome of a lost People's 77; Hungary 75, 78, 84–7; Islamification 78–9; migrants and minorities 10, 75–83; Muslim migrants 75–9, 81–2; myths 77–8, 83–4; national identity, threats to 75–6; no-go zones 78, 83–4, 87; nostalgia 77; Other 77, 79, 102; purity 77, 82, 84,
87–8; rhetoric 76, 84; securitization 75, 87–8; Sweden Democrats 3, 5, 75, 77, 79–83, 102; Swedishness 83; terrorism 76, 77, 82; Ukip 75, 79–83; uses of Swedish dystopia 79–83; utopia/dystopia, theories of 75–7, 80, 83, 88
Switzerland 8
Syria 42, 49, 78
Szél, Bernadett 58

Tambiah, Stanley 76
Taylor, Charles 76
Teitelbaum, Jonathan 6, 9, 35
temporalities 22, 29
terrorism 3; Belgium 53, 82; France 51; Hungary 51–2, 67–8; migrants and minorities 42, 45, 51–2, 56, 63–8, 76, 82–7; Norway 40; refugee crisis of 2015 51–2, 67–8; Sweden 76, 77, 82; Ukip 45; war on terror 52; white, right-wing terrorism 85–7
Thatcher, Margaret 11–12, 17, 30
Tibor, Szabó 63
Toroczkai, László 56
tourism 21
Towler, Gawain 34–5
training 34–5
traitors, liberal establishment as 86–7
Trollhättan, Sweden 85–6
Trump, Donald 1–2, 35–6, 40–2, 44–5, 68–9, 77, 102–4
Trump presidential campaign 5, 10, 35–6; *crimmigrants*, fear of 41; dual essentialization 45; essentializing white working class 41, 45; establishment and elites 41, 44–5; Hungary 68–9; masculinity 36; Other 102; radical Islam, war on 42; scapegoating 45; social media 41; Ukip 10, 35–6, 40–2, 44–5; white supremacy 45; whiteness and Americanness 46; working class 41, 44–5
Turkey joining EU, prospect of 82
Twitter 5–6, 41–2

UK Independence Party *see* Ukip
Ukip 1, 5; Breitbart advisers 40–2; Brexit 36–40, 42–6, 69; Britain First, disassociation from 34; civilization, threats to 10, 27–8, 35, 42–6, 82; climate change denial 31–2; crimmigrants, fear of 41–6;

demographic change 80–1; establishment and elites 26, 41, 43–5, 80, 101; EU 26–7, 36–40, 42–6, 69, 80, 103; Europe of Freedom and Direct Democracy grouping in EP 80; European Parliament elections 2014 80; fear, politics of 11, 41–3, 45; general election 2015, votes won in 22, 26, 80; image 34; inclusion, whiteness as basis for 10, 35; Islamophobia 42–5; mainstreaming 35, 38; media 34–5; migrants and minorities 27–9, 39–45; minorities, support from 27–9, 36–7; Muslim migrants 35–6, 42–4, 46, 80; nostalgia 8, 27–8; Other 102; post-industrial towns, targeting 8, 11–46; pro-coal platform 11, 22; professionalization 34–5; racialization 37, 45–6; racism and xenophobia 34–40, 45; rhetoric 42, 49; right, pushing politics to the 103; Sikhs 27–9, 46; social conservatism 22, 23; social media 5–6, 41; Sweden 79–83; training 34–5; Trump campaign 10, 35–6, 40–2, 44–5; violent imaginaries 42, 45–6; working class 38, 40, 42, 80; young persons 40–1; *see also* Doncaster, England, Ukip supporters in

unemployment: Hungary 54–5, 61, 63; Roma 54–5, 63; Ukip 11, 13, 14, 17, 23

United Kingdom: Britishness 27–8, 29; national identity 12; social media 5–6, 41 *see also* Brexit; Doncaster, England, Ukip supporters in; England; Ukip

United States: Charlottesville demonstration 36; Muslims, ban on entry of 36, 42; white settler state, US as a 35–6 *see also* Trump presidential campaign

utopia 75–7, 80, 83, 88

Vertovec, Steven 15
vigilantes 42, 87

violence: Hungary 9, 47, 57, 65, 84–7; imaginaries 10, 35, 42–7, 57, 65, 75–88; refugee crisis of 2015 47, 57, 65; Roma 102; Ukip 10, 42, 45

Vona, Gábor 42, 53–4, 56, 58, 61, 65–6, 69

wages, effect of migrants on 23
Wallace, William 19
waste *see* human waste/exception populations
wealth concentration and growth in metropolitan areas 15
welfare: chauvinism 24, 51; programmes 13
whiteness: Americanness 46; Englishness 37; families 68; gender 68; Hungary 9, 67–9, 85–7; inclusion, whiteness as basis for 35; masculinity 85–7; political correctness 35; refugee crisis of 2015 67–9; reterritorialization of whiteness 35; supremacy 35–6, 45, 80; Sweden 77; terrorism 85–7; Ukip 9, 10, 11, 15, 27, 29–30, 33, 34–46; working class 41, 45
Wilders, Geert 40
will of the people 2
Winberg, Kristina 80–1
women: feminism 5; Islam, status in 81; supporters of PRR 7; traditional roles 68 *see also* gender
Woolfe, Steven 36
working/lower class: authenticity 45; Brexit 44–5; Hungary 59; nativism 80; radicalization 45; resentment 3, 60; Sweden 80; Trump campaign 41, 44–5; Ukip 8, 11–29, 33, 36, 38, 40, 42; whiteness 41, 45
working men's clubs 18

xenophobia *see* racism and xenophobia

Yiannopoulos, Milo 35
young persons: Hungary 9, 60–1; Ukip 29–31, 40–1

Zionism 53–4, 56